SOCIALIST HISTORY SOCIETY

SOCIALIST HISTORY
OCCASIONAL PUBLICATION No. 28

BRADLAUGH
CONTRA MARX

RADICALISM VERSUS SOCIALISM IN
THE FIRST INTERNATIONAL

DEBORAH LAVIN

2011

Published by the
Socialist History Society
2011

ISBN 978-0-9555138-4-8

Designed and typeset by SHS, 2011
www.socialisthistorysociety.co.uk

Contents

1

Laura Lafargue (née Marx), 1870

Introduction: The Marx-Bradlaugh Conundrum

> ...it has been thought that ... myth-building ... was only possible because printing had not yet been invented ... on the contrary. The press and the telegraph, which spread their inventions over the whole earth in a second, fabricate more myths ... in one day than could formerly be done in a century...
>
> Karl Marx to Ludwig Kugelmann, July 27th 1871

The first full-length biography of Karl Marx was written early in the 20th century by John Spargo.[1] Born in Cornwall, Spargo had migrated to America, where, after some years of socialist activism, he deserted the labour movement and, perhaps because of this political apostasy, Spargo's book is not widely known or quoted, yet it has one specific advantage over later biographies. Writing in the very early years of the last century, Spargo was able to obtain some of his information directly from Marx's still-surviving second daughter, Laura.[2]

Although Laura had no independent political career of her own, she was held in great esteem within the international socialist movement, not only as Marx's daughter, but as the strong-minded and articulate consort of Dr Paul Lafargue, Communard,[3] founder member and leading figure of the Marxist French Workers' Party, the socialist deputy for Lille, journalist and author of, among much else, the ironic *The Right to be Lazy* and *The Religion of Capital*. In 1911, Lenin would speak at the Lafargues' joint funeral, where he conveyed the "deep feelings of sorrow" felt by the Russian Social-Democratic Labour Party (Bolsheviks) "on the death of Paul and Laura Lafargue". As she had none, Lenin could not say anything about Laura's political activity, but he described her husband as "one of the most gifted and profound disseminators of the ideas of Marxism".[4]

Laura spent her entire life among the leading figures of the international socialist movement; moreover she was very much her father's daughter, shrewdly observant and very willing to voice her own opinions. Engels claimed he went in fear of the young and beautiful Laura's icy stare.

Laura had metamorphosed into a plump elderly lady by the time Spargo approached her for family background material about Marx's life,[5] but pleased her father was finally getting a biography, Laura offered Spargo a host of anecdotes. One in particular hints at something significant, yet totally surprising to anyone immersed in the standard narrative of Marx and the International Working Men's Association (IWMA), which concentrates on Marx's successive battles against Mazzinista,[6] Proudhoniste[7] and Bakunista[8] attempts to infiltrate the IWMA, rather than his struggles with British radicals, let alone his battles with prominent secularists (Freethinkers) such as Austin[9] and George Jacob Holyoake,[10] or that "Individualist of Individualists"[11] Charles Bradlaugh. Yet, as Laura told Spargo:

> During the years 1857-58, the Freethought Movement under the leadership of Charles Bradlaugh developed great strength in London, where it had lagged since the forties. Bradlaugh gave a regular course of Sunday afternoon lectures not always directed against current theology, but often against political and social evils and abuses. Mrs Marx was a regular attendant at these lectures, always taking the two eldest children, Jenny and Laura with her. Marx also went on several occasions but he had little respect for the "Professional Atheist" and regarded the "Bishop of Atheism" as he called Bradlaugh with a good deal of aversion and suspicion. Mrs Marx on the other hand regarded Bradlaugh with great favour. She believed he would become a tower of strength to the working class movement. But Marx ... smiled at her enthusiasm and predicted he (Bradlaugh) would become the typical bourgeois liberal, a prediction which was amply fulfilled, Later on Marx fought desperately to keep Bradlaugh out of the International Working Men's Association.[12]

The image of Dr Karl Marx interrupting his studies and deliberately setting out one Sunday afternoon to go and listen to the now largely forgotten Charles Bradlaugh is unexpected. Yet even more startling is Laura's claim that Marx "fought desperately to keep Bradlaugh out of the International Working Men's Association". There were a great many radicals, non-socialists and even anti-socialists, among the initial members of the General Council of the IWMA, but while it is easy to understand why Marx would not want yet another one, especially one as large and bombastic as Bradlaugh, there is no immediate and compelling documentary evidence of any "desperate struggle" on Marx's part to keep Bradlaugh out of the IWMA.

Bradlaugh is hardly mentioned in the Marx-Engels Correspondence, or in the minutes of the General Council (or the smaller standing committee) of the IWMA. However, Laura is not completely alone in claiming that her father "fought desperately" to keep Bradlaugh out of the IWMA. In his memoirs, Frederick Lessner,[13] a longstanding personal friend of Marx and Engels and one of Marx's closest and most consistent supporters on the General Council, paints a picture very similar to Laura's:

...it must be put down as a great credit to Marx that he did all he could to keep the dubious self-seeking elements out of The International. In the early days all sorts of rag-tag including the High Priest of the Atheists, Charles Bradlaugh were milling around and it was mainly thanks to Marx that such people were given to understand that the International Working Men's Association was no nursery for religious or other sectarianism.[14]

Different as Laura and Lessner were in age and character, in their relationship to Marx and in their individual experience of the IWMA, there is no denying that they were both reliable witnesses and, despite the apparent lack of supporting evidence, their very clear and almost identical claims make their comments about Marx battling to keep Bradlaugh out of the IWMA worthy of serious attention. Although Bradlaugh's name rarely features either in the General Council minutes or in the Marx-Engels Correspondence, Marx most certainly made Bradlaugh the main topic of discussion at the meeting of the General Council of the IWMA held on December 19th 1871. To place the meeting in its context, this was six months after the fall of the Paris Commune and some nine months before The Hague Congress, when by successfully moving the General Council to New York, Marx and Engels in effect disbanded the IWMA or First International as it later came to be called.

The minutes of the December 19th 1871 meeting record Marx scathingly introducing his discussion of Bradlaugh by describing him as a "platform orator"[15] who had started his working life as "a clerk in some petty lawyer's office"[16] where he was given the opportunity to develop all the characteristic "low cunning of a solicitor's clerk"[17] as well as a "habit of falsification".[18]

In addressing these dismissive words to the members of the General Council, Marx was aware he was speaking to an audience familiar with Bradlaugh as a skilful speaker and energetic radical activist. Bradlaugh was president of the National Secular Society, which he had founded in 1866. More recently, Bradlaugh had founded the British Republican League. A supporter of manhood suffrage, Bradlaugh had also been a high profile member of the Reform League executive and had played a prominent part in a number of popular radical reform campaigns, from the long Free Speech fight to abolish "Taxes on Knowledge" (newspapers) to anti-Sabbatarianism and the abolition of the game laws.

Even so, Marx's hostile references to Bradlaugh's earlier non-political working life were well understood, as despite whatever merits Bradlaugh might have had as a radical campaigner, all the members of the General Council were very well aware that Bradlaugh was not only no friend of socialism, but he was also suspected of some rather murky dealings during the time he had worked as clerk to a now fugitive City solicitor, Montague Leverson.[19]

Leverson was a fraudster who had notoriously fled the country in 1867 to avoid what seemed an inevitable hefty prison sentence. Still, Charles Bradlaugh had only been Montague Leverson's employee, he was not Montague Leverson himself and Bradlaugh had recently and successfully sued a magazine for libel[20] when it suggested that as he had "been the clerk to a dishonest and fraudulent attorney" there was good reason to suspect Bradlaugh himself "was a dishonest person".[21] Bradlaugh had won the libel case, but he was only awarded derisory damages.[22] Bradlaugh could easily convince his followers and supporters that this outcome was the result of the jury's prejudice against him for his radicalism and militant atheism; yet for others Bradlaugh's reputation for sharp practice hovered in the background.[23] In the Victorian age as today there was discussion about how much of a man's private and non-political life should matter when assessing his politics; Marx's own position was unambiguously non-liberal. He utterly condemned the idea that "*la vie privée doit être murée*" as "infamous"[24] and he never had any reservations in making a connection between someone's political and non-political behaviour. Marx made no exception for Bradlaugh just as earlier in the year when he wrote the *Third Address on the Civil War in France*,[25] (an IWMA publication) Marx had had no reticence about drawing similar parallels between the public and private lives of "public men" when he discussed Adolphe Thiers, Jules Favre, Jules Ferry and the other prominent figures of the new Third French Republic.

Marx had begun the address by scornfully attacking the personal characters as well as the political horrors and humanitarian crimes committed by the victorious leaders of the new Third French Republic. Making his first written comments on Marx's *Address on the Civil War in France*, Bradlaugh, an opponent of the Commune and an admirer of Thiers, Favre and Ferry, attacked Marx in his weekly paper *The National Reformer*, for what he argued was Marx's gratuitous concentration on "personalities":

> We deeply regret to see a strong case weakened as we believe it to be by the introduction into the Address of coarse and useless personalities. Surely the references to Jules Favre's domestic relations cannot have the slightest force in enabling us to form a judgement on his conduct as minister of foreign affairs. That Jules

Ferry was penniless is surely an objection coming with ill grace from any writer on the popular side.[26]

With all the skills of an early 21st century tabloid journalist, Bradlaugh first praised Marx's style before going on to damn his content without actually discussing any of the central issues.

> Whatever opinions may be expressed on the merits of the case laid out in the pamphlet (*The Address on the Civil War in France*) it is impossible for even its most bitter opponent to deny that it has been written by a master pen ... As a philippic against Thiers the work of Dr Marx is terrible in its effectiveness but we doubt that Mr Thiers can have anything harder or more terrible said of him than he has of himself.[27]

Bradlaugh went on to concede that Marx's prose had all the "vivid fire" of William Cobbett and the "thoroughness" of Thelwell.[28] But this apparent praise was merely Bradlaugh's studied way of giving a patina of impartiality to his all-out attack on Marx. Bradlaugh would use the same technique whenever he commented on Marx's *Address on the Civil War in France*. He would always fulsomely praise Marx's style, before attacking Marx for dealing in what he called irrelevant "personalities". Taking just a few of Marx's sentences out of context Bradlaugh would boldly distort their meaning, always making sure that Marx's central arguments were derided without actually being discussed.

Bradlaugh's attacks were frequent and inevitably jarred on Marx; but in the aftermath of the fall of the Commune, Marx had many other concerns on his mind, and he gave Bradlaugh scant attention until he came to hear of a particular speech: *The Past, Present and Future of French Republicanism* which Bradlaugh had made on December 11th 1871 at the Hall of Science in Old Street. Variously described as an eight-hundred-seat or twelve-hundred-seat venue,[29] the Hall of Science at 142 Old Street was the London headquarters of Bradlaugh's radical powerbase, the National Secular Society. Bradlaugh spoke there regularly on Sundays to packed houses, but at this well-advertised meeting the audience overflowed.

Speaking just six months after the fall of the Paris Commune, Bradlaugh passed over the massacres of some 20,000 defeated Communards carried out by the victorious soldiery of Thiers and Favre, as well as the transportation for life of several hundred others to the penal colony of New Caledonia. Instead of any criticism of the new Third Republic, Bradlaugh roundly denounced the defeated Communards, not merely for their "impossible" socialist demands, but for "their" violence and "their" destruction of public buildings.

Ignoring the violence of the victors, while denouncing the violence of the defeated was a fairly standard "moderate" radical position. It was shared by several leading trade unionists, some of them original and leading members of the General Council of the IWMA – men such as George Howell[30] and George Odger,[31] who had also served with Bradlaugh on the executive of the now defunct Reform League.

If Bradlaugh had stopped with just another "moderate" radical attack on the Communards, Marx may well have ignored his December 11th speech; however Bradlaugh went far beyond merely attacking the Commune and defending the victorious Third Republic. He went on to make a savage personal attack on Marx and his *Address on the Civil War in France*.[32] Quoting, or rather misquoting Marx, Bradlaugh managed not only to deride Marx's understanding of economics, which Marx could easily have let pass, but he accused Marx of being a Bonapartist. As "evidence" to this claim, Bradlaugh used the following passage of Marx's in the *Address*:

> The natural offspring of the *party of order* republic was the Second Empire, with the *coup d'état* as its certificate of birth, universal suffrage for its sanction and the sword for its sceptre, professed to rest upon the peasantry the large mass of the producers not directly involved in the struggle between Capital and Labour. It professed to save the working class by breaking down parliamentarianism and with it the undisguised subservience of government to the propertied classes. It professed to save the propertied classes by upholding their economic supremacy over the working class; and finally it professed to unite all classes by reviving for all the chimera of national glory. In reality it was the only form of government possible when the bourgeoisie had already lost and the working class had not yet acquired the faculty of ruling the nation...

From this, Bradlaugh sententiously opined that Marx had made:

> ...two points here of grave error. One that the agricultural population have no interest in the wages question. Two, the declaration that the imperial government was the only form possible...

It was from this aside that Bradlaugh jumped to claiming Marx was a Bonapartist. Although clearly ridiculous to anyone familiar with Marx and his work, the assertion was actually plausible to Bradlaugh's audience at the Hall of Science. Made up of artisan radicals and social reformers rather than socialists, very few among Bradlaugh's audience were likely to have read anything Marx had written. Most would only know Marx as a name connected with the IWMA and this was an IWMA which had in the late 1860s steadily lost many of its leading trade unionist General Council members either to the Reform League agitation for Manhood Suffrage or to other non-socialist activities. More recently, after the fall of the Commune, the IWMA had lost two more of its best known radical General Council members, Benjamin Lucraft[33] and George Odger.

Lucraft and Odger both resigned after the publication of Marx's *Third Address on the Civil War in France* claiming the pamphlet was too supportive of the Paris Commune and that it should never have been issued as an IWMA publication. Haemorrhaging such well known men made it easier for Bradlaugh to represent the IWMA either as dangerous and extremist or as foreign-dominated and odd.

Bradlaugh's suggestion that Marx was a Bonapartist appeared very credible to the politically discontented, but confused, audiences who flocked to hear Bradlaugh pontificate at the Old Street Hall of Science. It was also very damaging and remained damaging even when Bradlaugh changed his accusation and, instead of damning Marx for being a Bonapartist, he damned him for being an agent of Bismarck.

Bradlaugh had never been a socialist, and while he had a hatred of the monarchy and the aristocracy, he could see no intrinsic conflict between capital and labour; and after attacking Marx and the Commune in equal measure he had ended his December 11th speech with a paean to class collaboration which played well to his radical artisanal audience, who could all recognise the injustices they witnessed all about them and wanted a fairer world, but as they took capitalism as a given, were easy prey to Bradlaugh's nostrums.

> Nations [Bradlaugh asserted] were not to be made up of one class, or another class, but of the people which included all classes (cheers). Here (in Britain) he desired a republic and would work for it, but if he could picture as the only possibility, the walking to its achievement with bloody hands, fire and smoke and grim visage, he would rather turn away now ere it was too late. Republicanism in France would have enough difficulty without class war. Her suddenly increased national debt made a burden not to be borne with impunity. Self-restraint was needed to conquer hate. Generosity on both sides. Amnesty for yesterday, peace for tomorrow and then a true republic might grow in the fair land of France. (Loud and continued cheering, several times repeated followed).[34]

Marx had no time to fight every outbreak of reactionary windbaggery, but when he was attacked by name before such a large audience, Marx felt he had no choice but to bring the issue of Bradlaugh to the General Council which met on December 19th 1871:

> Citizen Marx referred to the conduct of Bradlaugh, he said Mr Bradlaugh in a recent lecture with his usual fairness (sic) had tried to make it appear that he (Dr Marx) was a Bonapartiste, by quoting a passage (that was not given correctly), without giving the context from *The Civil War in France.* He (Marx) should not have noticed the matter, only there was the possibility of people being led astray by misrepresentation. On first reading the report (Marx) had had some doubt as to whether the misrepresentation was intentional. He thought it possible that Mr Bradlaugh was too stupid to understand the passage that in fact it was the result of incapacity rather than maliciousness... But on thinking over the matter; (Marx) had arrived at the conclusion that the falsification was deliberate and intentional ... it was easy to understand the man's malignity. He knew that (Citizen) Marx represented the labour struggle and that is why he vilified him, he knew that the International was struggling for the abolition of classes and that is what (Bradlaugh) dreaded. Some idea of a man might be formed by the company he kept...

Marx was finally gearing up to have a very public row with Bradlaugh, yet apart from a short discussion in Collins and Abramsky's *Karl Marx and the British Labour Movement*,[35] the 1871-1872 battle carried on by Marx and the General Council against Bradlaugh, fought out in the pages of the *National Reformer* and the *Eastern Post*[36] has been given scant attention by historians, socialist or mainstream alike. Neither Julius Brauthal in his *History of the International 1864-1914*,[37] nor David McLellan in his biography of Marx,[38] even so much as mention Bradlaugh, and other historians have simply followed suit.

Researchers into radicalism and socialism are in the habit of strictly adhering to their separate demarcated spheres and there has been very little appreciation that Karl Marx and Charles Bradlaugh lived in London at the same time, let alone that they were in conflict with each other as they competed to offer their alternative ideologies of radicalism and socialism to the same working class audience.

The National Secular Society

Bradlaugh's National Secular Society still exists as "the leading British pressure group speaking out for the rights of atheists, agnostics and all other non-believers".[39] The current NSS is a small middle class and intellectual organisation operating out of offices in Conway Hall, Holborn. But though the present day NSS boasts some very high profile honorary associates including, Richard Dawkins, Sir Terry Pratchett and Gore Vidal, its monthly journal has only a small circulation and most people would be hard-pressed to put a name to its current leadership.

In stark contrast, Bradlaugh's 19th century NSS was the biggest radical secular organisation in the country, with a membership dominated by the better off and aspirational artisan and skilled working class. This Victorian NSS had no well-known honorary associates, but it sustained Bradlaugh's weekly *The National Reformer* and in addition to its London headquarters at the Hall of Science in Old Street, it had a countrywide lecture circuit in all the major cities and several smaller towns besides. Made possible by the mid-century developments of the railways, this lecture circuit gave Bradlaugh's social and political pamphlets as well as his *National Reformer* significant additional outlets above and beyond the usual radical bookshops. It also provided a speed and regularity of distribution. What Bradlaugh thought and said in London was known within the week in all the populous industrial towns.

History has so reversed the respective fames of Charles Bradlaugh and Karl Marx that it is now difficult to grasp that among their British contemporaries Bradlaugh, not Marx, had the easier access to an audience and it was Bradlaugh, not Marx, who was the household name.

Ironically, Marx was more known among the political elite with access to confidential Home Office information on political refugees, than he was to members of the working class. In 1861, three years before the IWMA was set up, Lord Cranborne, later the Conservative Prime Minister, Lord Salisbury,[40] actually reviewed *Herr Vogt*,[41] one of Marx's lesser known works, archly describing it as:

> ...the invective of a refugee who lives in London (Marx) against a refugee who lives in Switzerland (Vogt). One of them has accused the other of being Napoleon's spy,[42] and the other retorts among other abuse with cutting observations on his adversary's personal appearance. It will add something to the secret history of 1848, and much to the vocabulary of any Englishman desiring to learn the art of German imprecation.[43]

As gratifying as it always is for a writer to be noticed, even by the Tory *Saturday Review*, Cranborne's mention did nothing to raise awareness of Marx among the British working class. And while English-speaking academics began to notice Marx from about the late 1870s onwards, John Rae's[44] assessment in 1881 of Marx's profile among British workers was painfully accurate:

> ...the country where Karl Marx is least known is that in which for the last thirty years he has lived and worked ... the writings of Marx in this country are hardly better known that those of Confucius ... and it is doubtful outside of a few radical clubs in London, the English proletariat so much as know his name.[45]

True, Marx was much better known in Europe; but even so, it needs to be properly taken on board that the worldwide and colossal fame of Dr Karl Marx was posthumous. In Britain throughout the 1860s and 1870s right up until the socialist revival of the early 1880s, Bradlaugh's works were far more accessible than those of Marx. And right up until the 1880s, it was extremely difficult, to the point of impossible, to locate copies of any of Marx's books or pamphlets in English, and in the days before large public newspaper archives, Marx's journalism was also fugitive.

Das Kapital published in German in 1867 was not translated into English until 1887.[46] As for Marx's shorter works, *Wages, Prices and Profit*, presented to the General Council of the IWMA in 1865, was not published in English until 1898. Yet it surely should have been printed immediately, as it successfully counters the common radical argument supported by Bradlaugh and defended in debate with Marx by General Council member, John Weston,[47] that strikes and other trade union activity could never raise wages as the amount of money available in the economy was fixed by an "iron law".[48]

The *Communist Manifesto* also spent most of the 19th century out of print and unavailable in English. Engels's *Socialism Utopian and Scientific* was not published in English until 1892.[49] And despite the controversy it caused, even Marx's 1871 pamphlet *Third Address on the Civil War in France* only had a print run of a few thousand.[50] In Britain, throughout Marx's lifetime, the unpalatable truth was that it was far easier for contemporaries to hear or read one of Bradlaugh's "falsifications"[51] of Marx's *Address on the Civil War in France* than it was to obtain and read Marx's *Address* itself.[52]

If Laura and Lessner were right and Marx did fight a "desperate struggle" to keep Bradlaugh out of the IWMA, the positions and relative fame of the two men meant that the battle was actually waged between a little-known political refugee with a small, if very intelligent and focused following, and a home-grown radical star with a massive fan club. Understanding this makes it far easier to realise why any "desperate battle" Marx fought to keep Bradlaugh out of the IWMA would be largely covert and hence difficult for the historian to trace.

Bradlaugh the Liberal MP

Marx was certainly right in thinking that the young firebrand Bradlaugh would end up as a typical bourgeois liberal. Bradlaugh actually spent the last years of his life as a Liberal MP, very much on the extreme and increasingly out-of-date *laissez-faire* wing of the party. In the late 1880s Bradlaugh would oppose the Workmen's Compensation Acts, the Shop Hours (Early Closing Day) Act and the statutory imposition of an Eight Hour Working Day, arguing that these were all interferences with free contracts between workmen and their employers. Bradlaugh also came out against London School Board proposals to give free dinners to the children of the capital's poor, using the standard Malthusian argument that helping poor parents feed their children would only encourage them to "over-breed".

By this time socialist and Fabian ideas were taking root and Bradlaugh was losing his previously strong grip on the working classes. He still had some lustre left from his previous more populist struggles, but it was perhaps best for Bradlaugh's posthumous reputation that he died when he did in 1891 as his name was allowed to sink into oblivion rather than disrepute. When Bradlaugh is remembered today, it is often quite favourably; his time as an extreme *laissez-faire* Liberal MP and his quarrel with Marx both lost to history. And Bradlaugh is usually only recalled for two political *causes célèbres* where he is generally seen by present-day civil rights and feminist historians as having played a heroic part.

These two *causes célèbres* generally known as "Bradlaugh and the Oaths Question" and *The Fruits of Philosophy* (or "Knowlton" Trial) took place some years after Marx's dealings with Bradlaugh and, at first glance, a detailed exposition of them might seem totally out of place in a discussion of Bradlaugh's interactions with Marx. Bradlaugh, however, and his significance as Marx's opponent, can only fully be understood if Bradlaugh's career is viewed in its entirety.

Bradlaugh, the Dubious Hero

The Oaths Question

Bradlaugh and the Oaths Question is invariably reported as if it were a civil or human rights issue which Bradlaugh had set out to confront deliberately. Nothing could be further from reality. What became known either as Bradlaugh's Oaths Question or sometimes as his six year "Parliamentary Struggle" came about by a combination of chance and misunderstanding, not a matter of principle.

Bradlaugh stood for Parliament in 1868, the year after the Reform League's original campaign for Manhood Suffrage had resulted in the 1867 Reform Act. Arguably the Reform League was the most successful single issue campaigning group of the 19th century. Set up in February 1865, it had only been in existence for just over two years before the Tory government passed the Second Reform Act, which, however, fell far short of the Reform League's initial demand for manhood suffrage, as the property qualifications ensured that only the better off working class were enfranchised.

The Reform League was formally headed by the Liberal barrister, Edmund Beales. The Liberal MP Thomas Hughes, author of *Tom Brown's Schooldays*, and Bradlaugh sat on its executive, along with a large number of IWMA General Council members. Initially, Marx was very enthusiastic about the Reform League, as he saw manhood suffrage as the necessary first step before an independent working class party could be set up and also because he saw the Reform League almost as an IWMA offshoot.

> The "International Association" (IWMA) has managed so to constitute the majority on the committee to set up the new Reform League that the *whole leadership is* (of the Reform League) in our hands.[53]

The Reform League executive certainly sounds like a roll-call of the early members of the IWMA's General Council: George Howell, George Odger, John Weston, Robert Applegarth, Peter Andre Fox, John Robert Taylor, William Stainsby, John D Neuss, Benjamin Lucraft, John Longmaid, John Bradford Leno, George Lake, George Milner, William Pigeon, George Wheeler, Edward Cousin, Robert Hartwell, James Buckley, James Carter, Cowen Stepney, William Cremer and William Dell. However, Marx was wrong in thinking that the sheer number of General Council members on the Reform League executive put the League "in our hands", as these men were not socialists, let alone followers of Marx. Most of them would resign from the General Council well before Odger and Lucraft resigned over Marx's *Third Address on The Civil War in France* and arguably, Marx only had good long-standing relations with three of them and these were problematical: Robert Applegarth,[54] who refused to sign off the *Third Address*, Peter Andre Fox,[55] a radical rather than a socialist, and Cowen Stepney, who was a friend of Holyoake.[56] Rather than having the "whole leadership" of the Reform League "in our hands", its leadership was actually more in the hands of radical opponents of socialism. Indeed, just a year after the Reform League was founded, Marx viewed it far more negatively:

> In England, the reform movement, which we brought into being, has almost killed us.[57]

Yet, while the Reform League leadership was radical rather than socialist, Marx along with Engels still supported its campaign, since gaining the franchise was unarguably an essential prelude to the foundation of a working class party. The radical Reform Leaguers, however, thought much more along Bradlaugh's lines than Marx's, and rather than set up an independent working class party, they actually hoped, in Engels's words, to form "...the tail (end) of the 'Great Liberal Party'".[58]

When the Reform Act of 1867 was followed by the 1868 General Election, rather than use the nationwide Reform League organisation as the nucleus of a new and independent working class party, the working class Reform Leaguers merely attempted to become adopted as official Liberal Party candidates, imagining that they could influence the Liberal Party towards a more working-class friendly agenda from within.

They were thwarted even in this humble aspiration by Gladstone and the Liberal grandees, who all eagerly sought the new working class vote, but were not interested in having working class candidates or even in making concessions to any working class demands, especially trade union reform. Almost as soon as the 1867 Reform Act passed, two very close associates of Gladstone, the MP George Grenfell Glyn[59] and Samuel Morley,[60] were tasked with suborning and manipulating the Reform League organisation and its accepted working class leaders with a view to winning the General Election without making any concessions to a working class agenda.

Glyn and Morley were remarkably successful. Using ex-General Council member, George Howell, as their principle agent and financial filter, the Liberals managed to win the General Election of 1868 without making any promises to the newly enfranchised artisan class. In effect, Howell and other working class leaders among the Reform League's executive were simply bought by the Liberal Party.

Relying on his powers of deductive reasoning rather than access to documentary proof, which he did not and could not, possess, Marx claimed at The Hague Congress of 1872 that "almost all" the recognised Labour leaders were "sold to Gladstone, Morley and Dilke". This was taken as a tremendous insult at the time; but Marx's assertion was true. Documentary details[61] have long since come to light which explain how in exchange, in effect, for ready money, Howell mobilised other working class ex-Reform Leaguers (and ex-General Council members) to deliver the working class vote to the Liberals, while keeping working class candidates off the ballot paper. Howell's own finances are revealing. Before his association with Glyn and Morley, Howell was a building worker with six pounds in his savings account, but after just eighteen months of working in the Liberal Party interest in the run up to the election of 1868, Howell was able to set himself up as a residential landlord.

While Howell and the vital role he played in delaying for an entire generation the creation of a purely working class party in Britain is of historical importance, what matters more directly to the narrative about Marx and Bradlaugh, is that in 1868 Bradlaugh wanted to stand as an official Liberal candidate for the town of Northampton, where he already had a following among the always very radical shoemakers of that predominantly shoemaking town.

As Gladstone did not want to see any working class candidates standing as Liberals, let alone any tub-thumping and militant atheist working class candidates, Bradlaugh was not selected. However, unlike the other disappointed working class ex-Reform League hopefuls, Bradlaugh did not meekly accept his fate and hope for another chance at a later date. Bradlaugh proved immune to all Howell's manipulations and blandishments, including Howell's trump card of loyalty to the Grand Old Man and the over-riding need for unity. Of course, Bradlaugh knew that if he stood against the two official Liberal candidates he would split the Liberal vote and perhaps even commit the cardinal sin of "letting the Tories in",[62] but Bradlaugh was not a man to put party, first last and always; so, when denied official Liberal Party backing, Bradlaugh stood as an Independent.

The two Liberal candidates still won but with a reduced vote. At the next General Election held in 1874 Bradlaugh was again denied official Liberal Party backing and again he stood for Northampton as an Independent. This time the Liberals lost one of the two Northampton seats in an election which brought Disraeli and the Conservatives into power. Even worse for the Liberals, the one remaining Liberal MP for Northampton died just a few months after the General Election. At the by-election held in October 1874, Bradlaugh again stood as an Independent and a Tory won what should have been a safe Liberal seat. When Bradlaugh threatened to stand once again as an Independent in the 1880 General Election, the Liberals were in effect cornered, so Gladstone caved in and allowed Bradlaugh to stand as an official Liberal candidate.

The High Anglican and fastidious Gladstone was very far from pleased at being outmanoeuvred by Bradlaugh and the actual prospect of having the militant republican atheist on his back-benches appalled him, but Gladstone knew there were some very simple ways of marginalising Bradlaugh. The Speaker, Henry Brand,[63] was both a Liberal and a friend of Gladstone's and once in Parliament Bradlaugh would surely find it difficult to "catch Mr Speaker's eye". Granted Bradlaugh would probably want to continue stumping the country expressing radical and atheistic opinions, yet perhaps tantalised with the prospect of junior office, even Bradlaugh could probably be prevailed upon to stump more quietly. In the normal course of events, Gladstone expected to be able to control Bradlaugh; however the normal course of events were interrupted, quite inadvertently, by Bradlaugh himself.

The Parliamentary Oath

At the beginning of each new Parliament, all MPs, unless they were Jewish or Quakers, swore an oath of allegiance to the Queen on the Bible; but on entering Parliament on May 3rd 1880, Bradlaugh asked Speaker Brand "to be allowed to affirm ... as a person for the time being by law permitted to make a solemn Affirmation or Declaration instead of taking an Oath".

Significantly, Bradlaugh, an avowed Republican and President of the short-lived British Republican League, recent author of an aggressive and well-published republican pamphlet *The Impeachment of the House of Brunswick*[64] did not foreshadow Sinn Fein, meaning Bradlaugh did not refuse to express his undying loyalty to Queen Victoria out of Republican principle, any more than he asked to affirm out of atheistical principle. He asked simply to affirm his allegiance to the Queen, rather than swear it on the Bible;

because he mistakenly thought that the right had already been granted to non-believers by the Further Evidence Act of 1869.

Bradlaugh was taken aback when Speaker Brand claimed he was unsure whether the Further Evidence Act of 1869 applied to the parliamentary oath as well as to oaths sworn in courts of law; and when the Speaker decided to set up a Select Committee to investigate the legal niceties, Bradlaugh did not stand on principle but, republican and atheist though he was, he offered to swear his allegiance to Queen Victoria on the Bible in the usual way.

Some prominent fellow secularists, including George Jacob Holyoake, sharply criticised Bradlaugh over this, arguing that Bradlaugh should have refused to swear on the Bible out of principle as an atheist. (Oddly, Holyoake made no mention of Bradlaugh's principles as a republican). Bradlaugh retorted that as swearing on the Bible was meaningless there was no harm in doing so, which rather called into question the long secularist crusade for the right to affirm in which Bradlaugh himself had played such a prominent part. This inter-secularist argument rumbled on in the pages of the *National Reformer* and up and down the country on the Freethought public platform. And on May 20th 1880, Bradlaugh had a letter published in *The Times*, where he explained to the outside world that he was willing to swear the oath on the Bible, as while:

> ...the oath to me (contains) words of idle or meaningless character ... my duty to my constituents is to fulfil the mandate they have given me, and if to do so, I have to submit to a form less solemn to me than the affirmation I would have reverently made. So much the worse for those who force me to repeat words which I have scores of times declared are to me sounds conveying no clear and definite meaning.

Bradlaugh's bold declaration offended many MPs and the House of Commons voted to deny him either the right to affirm or take the oath, which prevented him from taking his seat and voting in the Commons in the normal way of an MP.[65] In effect Northampton went unrepresented by its junior member which arguably made the case a constitutional issue, though no-one apart from Bradlaugh and his supporters treated it as such. Instead Lord Randolph Churchill saw the Oaths Question as a glorious opportunity to embarrass Gladstone.

Churchill, in Marx's words "a cheeky Tory youngster",[66] sought to create his Fourth Party out of the Bradlaugh Oaths issue. The quick-witted and highly opportunistic Churchill was interested in securing the working class vote for his emerging idea of radical

Toryism and in pursuing Bradlaugh and the Oaths Question; Churchill felt he had found a perfect way of dividing the Liberals from their already divided supporters. If Gladstone did not change the law to let Bradlaugh affirm and take his seat, he would alienate many of his new post-1867 Reform Act working class radical voters, but if Gladstone made the path easy for Bradlaugh, he would anger his core bourgeois Nonconformist vote, which was already furious that Bradlaugh had ever been allowed to stand as an official Liberal candidate in the first place.

The caricaturist Harry Furniss[67] gives a fair sketch of the superficial ins and outs of Bradlaugh's long parliamentary saga. Furniss is a hostile witness and he does not touch the *Realpolitik*, but he still writes vividly:

> Bradlaugh's bitter struggle would fill a volume. Select Committees were appointed, and they declared against him. Ignoring them, Bradlaugh marched up to the table and demanded to be sworn. The Fourth Party would not let him touch the Testament. Three days followed of angry debate on Bradlaughism, with more scenes. A new Committee reversed the decision of its predecessor, and said that Bradlaugh might affirm. Two days were consumed in discussing this, and the present Lord Chancellor, then Sir Hardinge Giffard, swayed the House against the report of the Committee. Nothing daunted, Mr. Bradlaugh the very next day was back at the table of the House, clamouring to be allowed to address the House on his case. A scene of wild confusion resulted, Mr. Bradlaugh endeavouring to speak, the House howling to prevent him. Eventually he was ordered below the Bar – that is, nominally outside the House, although within the four walls. After much acrimonious chatter from all sides, he was allowed to make his speech. His hour had come. He stood like a prisoner pleading before a single judge and a jury of 670 of his fellow-men. His speech was more worthy of the Surrey Theatre than of the "Best Club". It was bombastic and theatrical. He was ordered to withdraw, while the jury considered their verdict. When he was recalled, it was to hear sentence of expulsion passed on him. But he would not depart, and another tremendous uproar took place. Mr. Bradlaugh's well-trained platform voice rose above all others in loud assertion of his "rights", and he continued to call for them all through the House, the Lobbies, the corridors, up the winding stair into the Clock Tower, where he was immured by the Sergeant-at-Arms. The following day he was released after another angry debate, and he quickly returned to the forbidden precincts. Then he was induced to quit, but on the next day he came down to the House with his family, and with a triumphant procession entered the House amid the cheers of the crowd. So the drama went on day after day, like a Chinese

play. The characters in it were acted by the leading players on both sides of the House, and the excitement never flagged for a moment until Mr. Bradlaugh was allowed to affirm. He was told that he would vote at his own risk. He voted repeatedly, and by so doing incurred a fine ... nor could he even open his mouth in the House without savage interruption. Finally, Mr. Labouchère, his colleague, moved for a new writ for the borough of Northampton. Bradlaugh re-won the seat by the small majority of 132 votes, and the Bradlaugh incubus lay once more on Parliament. Then followed the same old cycle of events, the same scene at the table, the same angry religious warfare in debate ... the same speech from Mr. Bradlaugh at the Bar, the same division, the same result. Scene followed scene, and scandal for weeks, months, years.[68]

Furniss's sketch is accurate as far as it goes, yet Bradlaugh and his Northampton constituents did suffer an injustice. And Gladstone had it in his power to end the Oaths Question either by insisting that the Speaker should just allow Bradlaugh to swear the oath on the Bible in the normal way, or by passing a law specifically allowing MPs the right to affirm. At one point Gladstone, "that arch hypocrite and casuist",[69] decided to please the working class radicals and arranged for the House of Commons to have time to consider an Affirmation Bill. Gladstone even spoke in favour of affirmation but when the measure was defeated by three votes, he made no attempt to reintroduce it.

Yet, Bradlaugh remained Gladstone's loyal supporter, and though Gladstone was Prime Minister during the whole of what turned out to be Bradlaugh's six year "Parliamentary Struggle", Bradlaugh never directed any of his personal or political fury at the Grand Old Man.

Bradlaugh and the Oaths Question rumbled on, outside the House of Commons, as well as inside, with monster petitions, meetings and Trafalgar Square demonstrations, some of Chartist size. The Gordian Knot was finally cut in 1886 when the new Tory Prime Minister Lord Salisbury instructed Speaker Peel (a Liberal)[70] to end the furore; and on January 13th 1886, the atheist and republican Bradlaugh was finally allowed to swear his allegiance to Queen Victoria on the Bible in the usual way. Two years later in 1888 the Conservatives passed an Oaths Act, extending the right of affirmation from the courts to the parliamentary oath and the problem was done with once and for all.

The Tories' Oaths Act of 1888 is generally credited as a Civil Rights victory for Bradlaugh, but as he only got entangled in the Oaths Question by accident, and the moment he was allowed,

Bradlaugh willingly swore his allegiance to Queen Victoria on the Bible. It is surely quite erroneous to see Bradlaugh as playing the part of the heroic Man of Principle. Yet equally, no-one can deny that Bradlaugh was a man of extraordinary tenacity. Despite endless set-backs and humiliations, he just refused to give up, whether it was his twelve-year fight to be made an official Liberal candidate; or his six-year fight to be allowed to take his seat, Bradlaugh kept on battling. Nor can it ever be denied that Bradlaugh was able to keep a very large popular following loyal to him through all his vicissitudes. On different occasions during his six-year parliamentary struggle, Bradlaugh filled Trafalgar Square and the whole area around the Houses of Parliament with his supporters. Despite hordes of critics, including Marx and Engels, there were certainly many others among his contemporaries who felt a breathless adoration similar to that expressed by the young Henry Snell:[71]

> I have never been so influenced by a human personality as I was by Charles Bradlaugh. The commanding strength, the massive head, the imposing stature, and the ringing eloquence of the man fascinated me, and from that hour[72] until the day of his death, ten years later, I was one of his humblest but most devoted of his followers.[73]

Tenacity and popular appeal are attributes of considerable importance in Bradlaugh's earlier dealings with Marx. Once Bradlaugh had Marx in his sights his battle against him was not merely ferocious, it was, as will be shown, effective.

Bradlaugh's *Fruits of Philosophy* Trial

In direct contrast to Bradlaugh's accidental heroism of the Oaths Question, his earlier *cause célèbre* was a deliberately sought test case. In 1877, Bradlaugh along with a young and glamorous Mrs Annie Besant courted prosecution under the Obscene Publications Act 1857 by publishing with great fanfare and publicity *The Fruits of Philosophy, a manual for young married people* written by James Knowlton.

Bradlaugh and Besant wrote to the police telling them where and when and at what time they would personally be selling the book, which mixed Malthusian economics with practical birth control advice. They also sent copies of it to the City's solicitors at The Guildhall and to the heads of the City of London Police. They then sold it when and where they said they would sell it and were promptly arrested and charged.

Although *The Fruits of Philosophy* or the "Knowlton book" had been sold "under the counter" at radical bookshops for some forty years, just the year before in 1876, Bradlaugh and Besant's printer-publisher, Charles Watts had been threatened with prosecution after publishing a new edition with additional illustrative plates. To Besant and Bradlaugh's disgust, Watts, who had a wife and young children, "plea bargained". In exchange for pleading guilty, Watts was given a fine rather than a term of imprisonment. Bradlaugh and Besant broke with Watts over what they saw as this "cowardice", and early in 1877, they set up their own Freethought Publishing Company and immediately republished *The Fruits of Philosophy*. The outline of the story is well told by Annie Besant herself:

> An American physician, Dr. Charles Knowlton, convinced of the truth of the teaching of the Rev. Mr. Malthus, and seeing that that teaching had either no practical value or tended to the great increase of prostitution, unless married people were taught to limit their families within their means of livelihood – wrote a pamphlet on the voluntary limitation of the family. It was published somewhere in the Thirties – about 1835, I think – and was sold unchallenged in England as well as in America for some forty years. Philosophers of the Bentham school, like John Stuart Mill, endorsed its teachings, and the bearing of population on poverty was an axiom in economic literature. Dr. Knowlton's work was a physiological treatise, advocating conjugal prudence and parental responsibility; it argued in favour of early marriage, with a view to the purity of social life; but as early marriage between persons of small means generally implies a large family, leading either to pauperism or to lack of necessary food, clothing, education, and fair start in life for the children, Dr. Knowlton advocated the restriction of the number of the family within the means of subsistence, and stated the methods by which this restriction could be carried out ...The publisher of the *National Reformer* and of Mr. Bradlaugh's and my books and pamphlets had taken over a stock of Knowlton's pamphlets among other literature he bought, and he (Watts) was prosecuted and, to our great dismay, pleaded guilty. We at once removed our publishing from his hands, and after careful deliberation we decided to publish the incriminated pamphlet in order to test the right of discussion on the population question, when, with the advice to limit the family, information was given as to how that advice could be followed.[74]

Giving practical birth control advice is now seen as such an unambiguously laudable aim Bradlaugh and Besant's far from laudable motives for promoting contraception are rarely given the attention hey merit. While Bradlaugh and Besant express some interest in women's health and autonomy, these factors came a very distant second to their Malthusian economics. Following the dismal parson,[75] Bradlaugh had long believed and argued with all the passion of a Moses that in the almost unfettered capitalist society of mid-Victorian Britain, poverty was entirely due to the working class insistence on having "large families".

> The cause of low wages, or in other words Poverty, is over-population, that is the existence of too many people in relation to the food and of too many labourers in proportion to the capital ... Men starve because the bulk of them are ignorant of the great law of population ... the only possible mode of raising wages permanently and effectually benefitting the poor, is by educating them that their welfare depends upon taking such steps as shall prevent too rapid an increase in their numbers ... by ... checking (reducing) the supply of labourers.

Besant readily agreed with Bradlaugh's Malthusianism, as Malthus economic thinking was current in the Liberal Party circles in which she had been brought up.

Bradlaugh and Besant's position is now known as neo-Malthusian rather than Malthusian, as while they agreed with Malthus in seeing the high birth rate as the sole cause of working class poverty, they differed from him in the method of bringing the birth rate down. Malthus advocated reducing the working class birth rate by a combination of celibacy and late marriage. Bradlaugh and Besant argued that the working class birth rate could and should be reduced by a combination of early marriage and contraception.

Later as a Theosophist, Besant would renounce her neo-Malthusian views, but Bradlaugh remained a convinced neo-Malthusian until his death. In Bradlaugh's mind, nothing, not unions, not strikes, not workers' co-operatives or co-operation and certainly not legal enactment could alter the poverty-stricken conditions of the working classes, unless the workers decided to limit their own families by the use of "checks" or contraception.

Two years before the foundation of the IWMA, Bradlaugh's 1862 pamphlet, *Jesus, Shelley and Malthus*, compared Malthus's "manly" ideology of population reduction very favourably to Jesus's milksop "suffer the little children to come unto me" approach to human existence. Jesus, Shelley and Malthus was Bradlaugh's most popular and bestselling piece of outright neo-Malthusian propaganda, but he inserted neo-Malthusian sections into many of his other writings, and all during his editorship, *The National Reformer* continually featured articles on bourgeois "political economy" permeated with Malthusianism.

Neo-Malthusianism connected with the Victorian self-help and self-improvement ethos, which had an increasing purchase among the better off artisans and workers who were most interested and active in politics. It could even be seen as "empowering" as it put the solution to the problem of working class poverty, poor living conditions, lack of education and healthcare, squarely onto the broad shoulders of the working classes themselves.

Malthusianism is obviously opposed to Marxist ideas of surplus value and the reserve army of labour; and Marx attacked Malthusianism in detail in his major works. In passing he variously commented on Malthusianism as a "libel" on the intelligence and ingenuity of the human race and disparaged Malthus's "Population Question" as a bourgeois fantasy. Yet while Marx argued poverty was intrinsic to the capitalist system and would only end with its overthrow, Bradlaugh was winning vast audiences at the Hall of Science for his assertion that poverty would be abolished and a Capitalist Utopia installed if only working class women took to inserting a sponge before going to bed with their husbands.

If and when Besant and Bradlaugh's Malthusian underpinnings for supporting birth control are put to one side, it might be possible to present their determination to stand trial for publishing *The Fruits of Philosophy*, as a selfless and courageous act; and certainly civil rights commentators and feminist historians generally regard Bradlaugh and Besant as heroes for risking imprisonment by bringing *The Fruits of Philosophy* test case. However, just as the Oaths Question becomes less heroic under close inspection, the heroism of Bradlaugh and Besant's *Fruits of Philosophy* trial also appears dubious under scrutiny; as arguably, unlike Charles Watts or another of their colleagues, Edward Truelove, who was also prosecuted for selling *The Fruits of Philosophy*, Bradlaugh and Besant were never at any real risk of imprisonment.

Initially Bradlaugh and Besant were to be tried at the Old Bailey, but with all the technical and case knowledge of the law he had acquired during his days as Montague Leverson's clerk, Bradlaugh moved for trial at the Queen's Bench where the case would inevitably be tried by Lord Chief Justice Cockburn.[76] Bradlaugh's application was heard before Lord Cockburn and as Cockburn was well known for using his authority as senior judge on the Queen's Bench to ensure he took on all the most "remarkable" or "sensational" cases.[77] Men were regularly prosecuted for selling obscene publications, what made *The Fruits of Philosophy* sensational was the presence of a lady in the dock, and Bradlaugh knew enough about Cockburn to know that his application to move the trail from the Old Bailey to Cockburn's Queen's Bench would be successful.

Unusually for a High Victorian judge, Cockburn was known or his irregular private life (he had his own non-Malthusian reasons for supporting birth control). It was certainly no great surprise to anyone when Lord Chief Justice Cockburn summed up for an acquittal. However, although the judge proved tame, the jury surprised and returned a confused verdict of "guilty" with the rider that "we are unanimously of the opinion that the book in question is calculated to deprave public morals, but at the same time we entirely exonerate the defendants from any corrupt motive in publishing it".

The rider was meaningless in law, Cockburn had to act on the guilty verdict,[78] and he was forced to impose a prison sentence. Still, he allowed immediate bail (something not be granted Edward Truelove, when tried, not at Queen's Bench but at the Old Bailey for the same offence) and Bradlaugh and Besant's six-month gaol sentence was soon quashed on the technical grounds of there being a small inaccuracy in the original indictment.[79]

Overturning a conviction on a technicality was "one of those quibbles which by long-standing tradition were allowed to mitigate the horrible severity of our penal laws".[80] The practise was abolished by the 1915 Indictments Act, but in 1877, if a judge felt sympathetic towards the accused, he could overturn the jury's verdict (and the sentence he himself had imposed) with the excuse that there had been some small factual mistake in the original indictment. As such mistakes were common this amounted to a judge being able to act on a whim, even in capital cases.[81] Bradlaugh and Besant escaped imprisonment on just such a small quibble, which along with Bradlaugh's success in getting the case transferred to the Queen's Bench, begs the question of why, apart from the idiosyncrasies of Lord Cockburn's personality, Bradlaugh and Annie Besant should be treated so generously, when that very same year, their close associate Edward Truelove was not only tried at the Old Bailey rather than the Queen's Bench, but also denied bail, and made to serve a full four month sentence for the very same offence of selling *The Fruits of Philosophy*.[82]

The answer surely lies in a fact which has been previously passed over by historians, but which was so well known to Bradlaugh and Besant that it could not help but be part of their calculations. Unlike the various other *Fruits of Philosophy* defendants, James Watt, Edward Truelove (and Bradlaugh), Annie Besant *née* Wood came from a family with influential connections. Most significantly and usefully, one of her late father's cousins was a very recent Liberal Lord Chancellor, Lord Hatherley.[83] And while Cockburn and Hatherley were not exactly friends, they were very much part of the same close coterie of Liberal Party lawyers, all of them friends or close associates of Gladstone. By Annie Besant's own frequent admission, Lord Hatherley had proved very helpful to her on another occasion[84] and while no documentary evidence has surfaced to prove Lord Hatherley used his friendship networks to have his young and pretty cousin's conviction quashed, he can hardly have wanted to see one of his kinswomen facing the horrors of a mid-Victorian prison.

Granted *The Fruits of Philosophy* case was controversial, but controversy alone would not have prevented Lord Hatherley helping a relation. As a young man, he had been expelled from Winchester before going off to act as one of Queen Caroline's escort on her journey back to England to confront her husband, George IV. Queen Caroline was a radical cause and apart from her atheism, which he abhorred, Lord Hatherley was not necessarily hostile to Annie's views as chance would have it, one of Hatherley's favourite nieces, Kitty O'Shea,[85] would be Charles Parnell's mistress and while Hatherley would be dead before that particular scandal broke, rather than take the moral high ground, he would more than likely have supported Gladstone's pragmatic approach.[86]

Bradlaugh well knew of Annie Besant's kinship to Hatherley when he set out with her to court prosecution for publishing *The Fruits of Philosophy*. He also knew that as her co-defendant, whatever influence Hatherley might decide to use on Annie Besant's behalf, would inevitably be equally useful to him. In short, Bradlaugh and Besant's joint decision to make a test case out of publishing the Knowlton book lacked the heroism they claimed for it, as unlike Watts or Truelove, they were never in any real danger of imprisonment. In total contrast, Truelove's imprisonment for selling the book was very hard and very real.

The newspapers were full of the Besant and Bradlaugh *Fruits of Philosophy* case as well as Truelove's. Marx could not have escaped knowing about them; indeed he may have followed

Truelove's with a little interest as Marx had had some dealings with him. Truelove was a former Chartist, as well as a secularist and had been printer to the IWMA. It was Truelove who printed Marx's *Address on the Civil War in France*. There was another small connection, as at one time, the General Council of the IWMA held their Tuesday night meetings at Truelove's premises at 256 High Holborn. It is worth bearing in mind, when considering the Marx and Bradlaugh row, that Victorian radical and socialist London was a very small and interconnected town.

After *The Fruits of Philosophy* trial, Annie Besant decided to write her own neo-Malthusian birth control book, *The Population Question*, where she not only gave out incorrect advice as to the timing of the "safe period"[87], but in true Malthusian fashion she repeated *ad nauseam* the mantra that all poverty came from an excess of children. Besant even blamed the Irish and various Indian famines entirely on "large families" and "conjugal imprudence". *The Population Question* became a best seller. Estimates vary but it seems some 150,000 copies of Besant's book were sold within the first two years.

As Malthusianism and neo-Malthusianism alike were such anathema to Marx, Laura's claim that her father went to hear Bradlaugh speak could perhaps be doubted on that score alone; but timing is everything. Laura says her father went and heard Bradlaugh speak during the late 1850s and this makes sense. Bradlaugh was in his early to mid-twenties, and he had not yet written his absurd *Jesus, Shelley and Malthus* and though Marx would have inevitably recognised Bradlaugh as a radical with some very wrong and muddleheaded ideas, he may initially also have thought him capable of improvement; and besides, throughout the 1850s, Bradlaugh was often prominent in radical battles which Marx and other socialists could support such as the final push to remove the Taxes on Knowledge[88] and anti-Sabbatarianism.

Anti-Sabbatarianism

The importance of the long radical battle to remove taxes on newspapers is obvious; it made newspapers, the main media of the 19th century, more easily accessible to all but the very poorest; but Marx's interest in anti-Sabbatarianism requires a little more explanation. It became a major issue in the 1850s when under extreme pressure from the bourgeois Nonconformist and Evangelical Sabbath Day Observance Society legislation was introduced to enforce the 17th century bans on Sunday trading and entertainments. As an atheist, Bradlaugh opposed any legal enforcement of Sabbath-keeping, but he was also anxious to keep secularist lecture halls open on Sundays, as this was the only full day off that his working class audiences enjoyed. Although Marx recognised the anti-religious feeling against the Sabbath, he saw the proposed bans on Sunday trading and entertainment in class terms.

> The struggle against clericalism, like every serious struggle in England ... (is) assuming the character of a class struggle waged by the poor against the rich, by the people against the aristocracy, by the lower orders against their betters ... because the working class alone receives its wages late on Saturday... They are the only section of the population forced to make their small purchases on a Sunday and the Sunday Trading Bill is directed against them alone.[89]

But while Marx and Bradlaugh came at their opposition to Sabbath Day Observance from slightly different angles, they were most definitely on the same side in a struggle which was significant enough to result in riots in Hyde Park similar in size to the 1990 anti-Poll Tax or the 2010 student tuition fees riots.[90]

Bradlaugh was never personally a rioter, but he was physically a big man and he was very visibly present among the rioting throngs in Hyde Park (trying, he would later claim, to lead people away from the truncheon-wielding police to safety). As a recognised London working class leader, he was asked to give evidence at the Select Committee set up to look into the riots, and it was there, giving bold and swaggering answers, that Bradlaugh first really came to nationwide attention. It was a Bradlaugh newly made famous by the Hyde Park riots that Marx went along to hear.

Bradlaugh's anti-socialism

There was no *National Reformer* and no National Secular Society with its own headquarters at the Hall of Science at 142 Old Street when Marx with his young family in tow went to hear Bradlaugh speak at the old Owenite Hall of Science in John Street. At the time, Edward Truelove's bookshop and printing works was just next door and the area was something of a hub of "advanced thought".

There was invariably a crowd at the John Street Hall of Science, not only comprised of committed secularists, but old Owenites, O'Brienites and other utopians and active trade unionists, who, in the absence of a specific socialist platform, were willing to go and hear any good radical speaking against some current social evil which radicals and the more socialist-minded could unite in condemning.

These were the doldrum years between the collapse of Chartism and the inauguration of the IWMA. Socialism was in abeyance, but secularism was still associated with its early ideas of co-operation and utopianism as well as land reform and the old Corresponding Society demands for constitutional change. And even though young Bradlaugh was loudly proclaiming his belief in birth control, this demand was not always immediately seen as Malthusian. Some radicals supported contraception out of a feminist concern for women's health. In this eclectic but dissident milieu, Bradlaugh's support for a wider franchise and republicanism along with his various attacks on particular government policies went a long way towards disguising his visceral anti-socialism.

Bradlaugh's anti-socialism really only began to separate him from the working classes in 1884, the year after Marx's death, when, H M Hyndman[91] challenged Bradlaugh to debate the question "Will Socialism Benefit the English People?"[92] Hyndman decided to confront Bradlaugh at the outset as he recognised him as a beast too big to be ignored:

> Bradlaugh was undoubtedly the most formidable and imposing platform figure in the country. An individualist of individualists... that every man must make his own way with his own right arm... [that] the weakest must go to the wall was (to his mind) a beneficial fact for the race, (that he himself), would survive... As one of the fittest he had no doubt and [Bradlaugh] took good care to impress that view with all who he came into contact.[93]

In the 1884 debate, Bradlaugh used the same techniques against Hyndman as he had earlier used against Marx. While Hyndman, like Marx, argued first principles:

> What is Socialism? ... Socialism then is an endeavour to substitute for the anarchical struggle or fight for existence, an organised co-operation for existence.[94]

Bradlaugh picked up and twisted peripheral details:

> How, [Bradlaugh asked] when the State owns railways, is it to be managed? May I go to Aberdeen if and when I please? Omnibuses and cabs, how are they to be regulated when the collective property belongs to the organised State? How will you get your cabmen and chimney-sweeps? If you organise labour, you must pick all these men, and who is to be the "you" to pick them? How is the distinc-

tion to be made between employment on skilled and unskilled labour?[95]

When Hyndman responded by stating that in an evening's debate it was impossible to account for every "cabman and chimney sweep", Bradlaugh raised an easy laugh by condemning Hyndman for claiming to speak for the working class while having no interest in "cabmen and chimney sweeps". Bradlaugh ended the debate with a statement of his own position:

> The distinction between myself and my antagonist is this... we both recognise many social evils. He wants the State to remedy them; I want the individuals to remedy them.

Although this April 1884 debate took place four years into the Oaths Question when Bradlaugh could still command crowds of supporters and the evening has generally been hailed as a Bradlaugh victory, the Hyndman-Bradlaugh debate marked the beginning of Bradlaugh's personal eclipse. However, his radical, self-help and Malthusianism ideas unfortunately still live on and Bradlaugh's earlier battles with Marx also have modern parallels well worth considering.

H M Hyndman

Bradlaugh and the IWMA

Bradlaugh and the General Council

The absence of any significant mention of Bradlaugh either in Marx's correspondence or the IWMA minutes before Marx and Bradlaugh's public row in 1871 tends to suggest that Laura and Lessner must be wrong in thinking Marx had a battle on his hands to keep Bradlaugh out of the IWMA. But Bradlaugh himself comes forward offering information which gives substance to Laura and Lessner's allegations.

The National Reformer for October 8th 1865 reports that Bradlaugh attended the soirée at St Martin's Hall on September 28th,[96] held by the IWMA to celebrate its own first anniversary and Abraham Lincoln's freeing of the slaves in the United States earlier in the year.

The soirée was a large, well-attended event, its size showing very clearly how mainstream the early IWMA was intended to be in working class politics. There was a full report of the event in the IWMA's current official paper *The Workmen's Advocate*. The text is too long to quote in full, but a few excerpts are illuminating:

> The hall was most appropriately decorated with flags of the different nationalities, the place of honour being assigned to the Stars and Stripes of America... Over 300 sat down to tea... Tea being over Citizen Odger (the IWMA President) was called to the chair... He concluded by an earnest appeal to the meeting, and to the country through the press, to forward the progress of the Association, whose object was the enfranchisement of all nations, and the elevation of our common humanity. (Cheers.)... The President [Odger] then called on Citizen Cremer to propose the adoption of the Address to the People of America... Mr. Charles Bradlaugh, in seconding the adoption of [Cremer's] address, said... He deeply sympathised with the sentiments of the address and with the objects of the Association generally. Not only had they the American flag over their heads, but he could see one mutely expressing their deepest and most earnest longings – the freedom of Venice and Rome. (Loud and long continued cheering.) To effect universal liberty, men must know their duties and take their rights. There must be something higher in our aspirations than mere nationality. To live on the banks of the Po, the Seine, or the Thames does not confer the right to greatness or freedom. No; it must be honesty, integrity, and ability. We must not suffer crowned heads to use us as tools for their own purpose and the oppression of other peoples. Yet so they have used us in the past: let it never return. (Cheers.) The gilded thing called a crown could in a mo-

ment be pulverised by the strong, stern arm; yet in its hesitation its strength is lost, and the bauble resumes its power over the weak, the superstitious, and the ignorant, and by the aid of the self-interest of court parasites, again oppresses the people. (Cheers.) Let them be true to their principles, and these things will become a thing of the past, and truth and justice will triumph. (Applause.)

Bradlaugh's windy Mazzini-like speech would not have endeared him much to Marx, but Marx was not at the soirée as he had gone to visit Engels in Manchester. If Marx had been present he might have prevented Bradlaugh speaking as though the *Workman's Advocate* does not mention it, Bradlaugh was not billed as a speaker; and he was only asked to second Randal Cremer's address because Ernest Jones[97] had failed to appear. Such formalities mattered in the culture of the working class movement. The very fact Bradlaugh was chosen to stand in for Ernest Jones meant that Bradlaugh was considered a significant working class leader by the IWMA members present.

The evening continued:

> At the conclusion of the speeches a very large and handsome tri-coloured flag was hung over the end gallery with the following names – Italy, Poland, Hungary, Mazzini, Garibaldi, which created an immense burst of cheering, which was again and again repeated.
> [The] music and singing by the Garibaldian Band and the German Working Men's Choir, which gave the Marseillaise and other pieces with much effect... The hall was then cleared for dancing, which amusement was followed up with much spirit for some hours... At two o'clock the Committee and delegates assembled in the Committee room, where Citizen Cremer was most warmly received, and the thanks of the delegates accorded to him for the able manner in which the soirée had been got up and the splendid success they had that night witnessed.

The National Reformer also reports the soirée as a great success, but in contrast to *The Workman's Advocate* which makes no reference to Ernest Jones's failure to appear, *The National Reformer* makes great play of it and specifically claims that Bradlaugh was invited to stand in for the absent, and well respected, Jones.

The National Reformer had a breathless, self-important style, rather reminiscent of Charles Dickens's satirical description of the meetings of the Pickwick Club a generation before. Not content with merely claiming that Bradlaugh made a good speech which was well received, *The National Reformer* proclaims that Bradlaugh made a "magnificent speech", which had the whole gathering "in raptures":

> Mr Bradlaugh's eloquence produced a thrilling effect on the numerous audience and after a splendid speech, frequently interrupted by repeated applause...

The National Reformer then reveals what is recorded nowhere else:

> Mr Bradlaugh confessed that he had been guilty of not taking the card of membership till that evening but now that he was a member [of the IWMA] he meant to work for the association...

This apparently excited the audience into even more extreme "raptures", but finally:

> Mr Bradlaugh sat down among a thunder of applause.

In September 1865, Bradlaugh was thirty-two. He was still over a year away from setting up the National Secular Society; three years away from possessing the 800 to 1400 seat Hall of Science in Old Street. He was not even the editor of *The National Reformer* but if he had not been seen as important, he would not have been offered a seat on the Reform League, as he was earlier in the year, nor would he have been asked to stand in for Ernest Jones. Bradlaugh never joined organisations merely to remain a rank and file member and with so many of his fellow members of the Reform League executive also sitting on the General Council of the IWMA, Bradlaugh confidently expected the public announcement of his decision to join the IWMA to be treated as momentous and that he would immediately be offered a seat on the General Council.

The General Council minutes of the IWMA are sparse. Details of important debates and quarrels are frequently omitted with only a tantalising "a discussion took place" hinting that there was any discord or disagreement; however despite their other failings, the minutes scrupulously record the nomination and election of new members, yet at the General Council meeting held immediately after the soiree, Bradlaugh's name is not mentioned. Instead there is the mysterious sentence:

> A discussion took place as to the late soirée... An explanation having been given, the subject [was] dropped.[98]

Marx was back from visiting Engels in Manchester and present at this General Council meeting, so was Victor Le Lubez.[99] Le Lubez was very close associate of Bradlaugh and for a long time Le Lubez served as treasurer of the National Secular Society. Ironically, it was Le Lubez who had first called on Marx asking him to come to the inaugural meeting of the IWMA to be held on September 28th 1864 at St Martin's Hall. Le Lubez approached Marx simply because Marx was a German 1848er; he certainly had little idea that Marx's political thinking conflicted with that of his hero, Bradlaugh.

> A certain Le Lubez was sent to ask me if I would participate *pour les ouvriers allemands* and, in particular, whether I was willing to provide a German worker to speak at the meeting, etc. I provided them with Eccarius, who put on a splendid performance, and I was also present myself in a non-speaking capacity on the platform...[100]

As someone close to Bradlaugh, Le Lubez was also an admirer of Mazzini, and Marx immediately came into conflict with Le Lubez during the drawing up the IWMA's rules and regulations. Marx prevailed and nearly all the Mazzinista elements that Le Lubez and other Mazzini supporters, including Luigi Wolff, had inserted were removed from the final text, but rancour remained. In the months that followed, Marx managed to get Le Lubez removed from the pivotal position as correspondence secretary for France and then finally expelled from the IWMA at the Geneva Congress in 1866.

Knowing Le Lubez was entwined with Bradlaugh, Laura and Lessner would have seen Marx's battle to get Le Lubez out of the IWMA as part of his "desperate struggle" to keep out Bradlaugh, a connection lost on anyone unaware of the links between Le Lubez and Bradlaugh.

Logically Bradlaugh would be expected to be nominated to the General Council immediately (or at least very soon), after he had very publicly taken out membership and committed himself to working for the IWMA. There might reasonably be a delay of a meeting or two, but while the General Council minutes record all other nominations there was never any mention of Bradlaugh being nominated, let alone elected onto the General Council of the IWMA. After Bradlaugh's October 8th 1865 announcement in *The National Reformer* that he had joined the IWMA and intended to work for it, there is no further reference to Bradlaugh ever having attempted to join. It is not in *The National Reformer* nor anywhere else.

A close study of the General Council minutes shows only a handful among the scores of nominees ever being rejected, yet two of the refusals were of very close associates of Bradlaugh. These were the prominent Secularist brothers, Austin and George Jacob Holyoake. Austin Holyoake died in 1874, when he was still working closely with Bradlaugh; George Jacob Holyoake lived on to spectacularly fall-out with Bradlaugh over *The Fruits of Philosophy* Trial and the Oaths Question. But like his brother Austin, at the time George Jacob Holyoake tried to join the General Council his working relationship Bradlaugh was at its closest. Marx most certainly kept out George Jacob Holyoake and the suspicion must be that he also kept out his brother.

Indeed a pattern can be seen emerging of Marx keeping the "professional atheists" out of the IWMA; yet ironically, years later, Marx was accused by another early and leading General Council member, George Howell, of doing just the opposite. Against the evidence, Howell dishonestly claimed in an article in the *Nineteenth Century*, July 1878, that Marx introduced what Howell called the "religious idea", or the issue of atheism, into the IWMA.

Marx vociferously denied Howell's allegation, but as he was refused the right to reply by James Knowles, the editor of *Nineteenth Century*, Marx could only rebut Howell in the much smaller circulation *Secular Chronicle*,[101] which was owned and edited by Harriet Law.[102] A non-Bradlaugh secularist, Harriet Law had sat on the General Council from 1867 where she had consistently supported Marx; and despite her own militant atheism, Mrs Law often prioritised socialism over secularism. In the interest of fair play and loyalty to Marx she allowed him to defend himself against Howell's intentionally damaging and charge of, in effect, having divisively suggested atheism should be made a condition of IWMA membership: Quite the contrary, Marx explained:

> The programme of the General Council contained not one syllable on "Religion", but at the instance of the Paris delegates the forbidden dish got into the bill of fare ... for the prospective Congress ... The topic of discussion (Religion) thus introduced by the Paris delegates was left in their keeping. In point of fact, they dropped it at the Geneva Congress of 1866, and no one else picked it up.

Marx then made this point about his and the IWMA's attitude to religion and atheism:

> The attitude of the General Council in regard to the "Religious Idea" is clearly shown by the following incident: – One of the Swiss branches of the Alliance, founded by Michael Bakunin, and calling itself *Section des athées socialistes*, (Section of Socialist Atheists) requested its admission to the International from the General Council, but got the reply: "Already in the case of the Young Men's Christian Association, the (General) Council has declared that it recognizes no theological sections."

Denying entry to the YMCA and Bakunin's supporters as "theological sections", indicates that Bradlaugh's National Secular Society would have been denied entry on exactly the same grounds. And in truth, despite Howell's provocative claim in the *Nineteenth Century*,[103] Marx opposed all moves to adopt atheism as a condition of IWMA membership, as despite being as much an atheist as Bakunin, Marx believed that making atheism compulsory would only alienate large swathes of the working classes, Catholics and Protestants alike.

Marx's youngest daughter Eleanor records her father taking her to the local Catholic Church to listen to the "beautiful music", and once quite sentimentally telling her that "...after all we can forgive Christianity much, because it taught us the worship of the child".[104] And in a couple of the surviving pictures of Marx's other two daughters, Jenny and Laura, the two young women are clearly wearing Catholic crosses. Jenny and Laura were as atheistic as their father, and wore the crosses to show their solidarity with Ireland and Poland rather than Christianity,[105] nevertheless really militant atheists like Charles Bradlaugh, do not, as a rule, pop into churches to listen to the music, wear crosses or talk mawkishly about the Christ-child.

Still Marx was hardly a great friend of the "opium of the people" and he certainly never imposed a blanket ban on individual secularists in the IWMA. He just did not want people on the General Council to prioritise atheism, as Bradlaugh would have done. Marx was happy to support the nomination of the secularist, Harriet Law, onto the General Council, because he viewed her commitment to socialism to be as strong as her commitment to secularism. Marx also worked well with another fairly prominent secularist, Peter Andre Fox;[106] since even though Fox was not a socialist, his interest in "the social question" was pushing him in that direction before his early death in 1869. Marx also got on reasonably well with Stepney Cowen, even though was friendly towards George Jacob Holyoake.

George Jacob Holyoake was active in the Co-operative as well as secularist movement (and Cowen liked him more for this reason) but like his brother Austin, nominated for the General Council as early as November 8th 1864, George Jacob Holyoake's commitment to secularism could sometimes over-ride his other interests.

Austin Holyoake was Bradlaugh's printer and was very closely aligned to him politically. Austin Holyoake's nomination to the General Council was mentioned once and then disappeared mysteriously into the historical ether, never to surface in the minutes again. This is almost unique. Nearly all nominations successfully proceeded to election and the few rejected nominations are almost always explained. The strange disappearance of Austin Holyoake from the IWMA minutes may well be another example of

Marx's struggle to keep Bradlaugh's supporters out of the IWMA, but there is no conclusive documentary evidence.

Happily, there is some evidence to show Marx deliberately excluded George Jacob Holyoake from the IWMA. Loosely speaking, George Jacob Holyoake was the biggest figure in secularism after Bradlaugh. Until Bradlaugh arrived in force in the early 1860s, George Jacob Holyoake had been seen as the leader of the secularist movement, but he was a poor public speaker with a thin, weak voice, and, with the advent of the more formidable Bradlaugh, George Jacob Holyoake found himself marginalised. Still, while there were periods of fierce hostility between Bradlaugh and George Jacob Holyoake, all importantly, in November 1869 when George Jacob Holyoake made his attempt to get onto the IWMA's Central Council, he and Bradlaugh were enjoying one of their longest periods of harmony. George Jacob Holyoake could even be described as Charles Bradlaugh's "New Best Friend".

The General Council minutes are only a little less tight-lipped about George Jacob Holyoake's application than they were when Austin Holyoake and Charles Bradlaugh had both tried to join four years previously, but luckily this time Marx wrote to Engels for advice about what he termed "an incident" at the last General Council meeting:

> Mr Holyoake... appeared and after leaving, had himself proposed by (John) Weston (who) tentatively declared that (George Jacob Holyoake) should first take out a card as a member of the International Working Men's Association, (so that he could be formally) proposed (for membership of the Central Council). [107]
>
> Holyoake's aim is simply to make himself important – and to figure as a delegate at the next General Congress. The debate on his admission will be stormy, since he has many friends among us and, as an offended intriguant, could play some nasty tricks on us. What are your ideas about the tactics to be followed?

Engels thought the Holyoake issue important enough to reply by return of post:

> The business with Holyoake is vexatious. The fellow is simply a go-between for the radical bourgeoisie with the workers. The question is this: is the composition of the General Council such that a swamping by such rabble is to be feared or not? If you accept Holyoake, then others might follow, and they will do so as soon as the affair becomes more important. Moreover, if the times become more tempestuous, these gentlemen will certainly also visit the sessions, and try to grasp the leadership. And as far as I know, Mr Holyoake has never done the slightest thing for the working class

as such. A priori, everything against his acceptance, but if his rejection would lead to splits in the Council, while his acceptance would, in practice, make little difference to the constitution of the General Council, *eh bien.* Despite this I cannot well envisage a workers' Council with this fellow on it.

Essentially with George Jacob Holyoake, as with Charles Bradlaugh and even Austin Holyoake, Marx faced the age old political dilemma, which President Lyndon B Johnson described with cowboy clarity when he was wondering what to do about J Edgar Hoover of the FBI. Was it was safer, Johnson wondered, to have your enemies inside the big tent, spitting out, or outside spitting in. Johnson came down on the side of having J Edgar Hoover come inside and spit out, but despite Marx's very real fears that George Jacob Holyoake had "many friends among us and as an offended intriguant, could play some nasty tricks on us" Marx chose the alternative option. Marx kept George Jacob Holyoake out. As Holyoake was Bradlaugh's bag-man at the time, Laura and Lessner's claim that Marx was instrumental in keeping Bradlaugh and his followers out of the IWMA, does now seem to have put on some serious flesh.

Even so, before Marx's row with Bradlaugh over the Paris Commune in 1871, Marx was very still far from being obsessively anti-Bradlaugh and as late as November 29th 1869, when both George Odger and Bradlaugh were suggesting themselves as Liberal Party candidates for the constituency of Southwark, Engels saw no problem in suggesting to Marx that:

> It would be very fine to get Odger into a hole. I hope Bradlaugh will stand for Southwark as well as he, and it would be much better if Bradlaugh were elected.[108]

Marx may have taken Engels's comment as more anti-Odger than pro-Bradlaugh, but whatever way he took it, Marx did not find it important enough to rebut. As it happened, Engels's expressed preference was redundant as Howell's clandestine organisation, well-funded as it was by Glyn and Morley, made very sure neither Odger nor Bradlaugh became official Liberal Party candidates for Southwark.[109]

Interestingly what this makes clear is that having successfully kept Bradlaugh and several of his important followers out of the IWMA, Marx did not consider Bradlaugh any kind of on-going threat, rather it was if Marx felt Bradlaugh and his acolytes had been successfully dealt with; which is perhaps why Marx rejected out of hand the overtures made by a group of anti-Bradlaugh secularists to set up an organisation opposed to him and the *laissez-faire* cum Malthusian views he was infiltrating into the previously progressive secularist movement. As Marx wrote to Engels:

> Enclosed letter from Maughan,[110] man of private means, old Owenite, very decent fellow. These people are obviously intending to emancipate the freethinker movement from the professional agitators Bradlaugh, etc. I very politely declined. On the one hand, it is true that I would thereby have had the chance, which I am wanting so much, of becoming acquainted with all manner of people who are to a greater or lesser extent, directly or indirectly, connected with the English press. On the other hand, I have not the time, nor do I think it right that I should figure on the leading committee of any English sect.

Marx may well have been rather too confident in thinking that a specifically anti-Bradlaugh organisation was something he could safely leave to others. In the latter part of the 1860s Bradlaugh's position as a member of the Reform League executive gave him constant contact with all the twenty-odd IWMA General Council members who also sat on the Reform League's governing body. While Marx carefully avoided being elected IWMA president or secretary and he made sure that public pronouncements and addresses were made in the name of the entire General Council, Bradlaugh received regular insider information about Marx via the joint Central Council-Reform League executive members. And truth was, while Marx may have taken his eye off Bradlaugh, Bradlaugh was keeping a very watchful and very hostile eye on Marx.

Bradlaugh and "Violence"

Although Mazzini's woolly religiosity logically conflicted with atheism, British radical secularism made a cult of Giuseppe Mazzini. Edward Truelove even gave the name Mazzini to his son.[111] Bradlaugh was on very good and friendly terms with all the Italian (and non-Italian) Mazzinistas on the General Council. As eliminating Mazzini's influence was Marx's first ideological battle within the IWMA, Bradlaugh inevitably soon became aware that Marx did not share the general British radical admiration for the Italian patriot.

In a letter Marx wrote to Engels on November 4th 1864, he told a rather sceptical Engels about his success in wresting control (not just from Le Lubez but all Mazzinistas) of the important task of writing the IWMA's initial *Address to the Working Classes* as well as the general rules. Marx was correct in describing it as a coup. Marx had missed a couple of the early meetings where the rules were being drawn up and Le Lubez and the other Mazzinistas on the central council had come up with a confused,

> fearfully cliché-ridden, badly written and totally unpolished preamble pretending to be a declaration of principles, with Mazzini showing through the whole thing from beneath a crust of the most insubstantial scraps of French socialism.

Eliminating Mazzini's romantic, class-collaborationist and nationalist ideology was a notable victory for Marx at the IWMA's outset; but it was not necessarily accepted as permanent and final by the defeated. Bradlaugh may even have decided to take out membership of the IWMA at the October 1865 soirée to give added weight to the Mazzinistas' fight back. Bradlaugh's exclusion could be viewed as another defeat for the Mazzinistas. It is certainly noticeable that the Italian supporters of Mazzini did not leave the IWMA *en masse* until after Bradlaugh's application to join had been "disappeared". Meanwhile, Bradlaugh remained in regular contact with Le Lubez and any other non-Italian Mazzini sympathisers.

A close look at Bradlaugh's networking patterns outside the secularist movement reveals he was strangely drawn to anyone with any level of conflict with Marx. Apart from the Italian Mazzinistas and their many English sympathisers, Bradlaugh also courted the London French headed by the opponent of Marx, Felix Pyat.

Initially the London French were IWMA members who came to London to escape Napoleon III's renewed onslaught in the mid and late 1860s against political dissidents of every stripe. There were so many of these refugees from the Second Empire that it was impossible to accommodate them all on the General Council and they set up the London French as their own IWMA sub grouping. This was an innovation. Alone among the countries making up the IWMA, Britain did not have provincial or any other kind of federal section. Marx and his allies were adamant that the General Council could do double duty in Britain and function as both the national organisation for Britain and the central committee for the entire IWMA. This position became increasingly untenable and was finally abandoned in the IWMA's dying days.

As to the London French, for a while Marx's two future sons-in-law, Charles Longuet and Paul Lafargue (both political fugitives from Napoleon III's France) considered themselves members, but they were also members of the General Council and they broke away completely from the London French when Felix Pyat[112] took over leadership of the group. It is a complex story which perhaps Marx outlines best:

> Some time ago I promised to write you a few words about the French Branch. These ragamuffins are, a half or 2/3 of them, *maquereaux* (pimps) and such-like rabble, and all of them – after our people had withdrawn[113] – heroes of the revolutionary phrase, who, from a safe distance, of course, kill kings and emperors, in particular Louis Napoleon. In their eyes we are, naturally, reactionaries, and they drew up, in all due form, an indictment against us, which was, in fact, submitted to the Brussels Congress – in the closed sessions. The fury of these blacklegs was heightened by the fact that they had been taken over by Felix Pyat, a failed French fourth-class author of melodramas... a man who has a perfect monomania "to shout in a whisper" and to play the dangerous conspirator. Pyat wanted to use this gang to convert the International Working Men's Association into his following. In particular, the aim was to compromise us. Thus, at a public meeting which the French Branch announced and trumpeted by poster as a meeting of the International Association, Louis Napoleon, alias Badinguet, was in all due form sentenced to death, the execution naturally being left to the nameless Brutuses of Paris. Since the English press paid no attention to this farce, we also would have passed it over in silence. But one of the gang – a certain Vésinier,[114] a circulator of *chantange* (blackmail) literature – spread the whole muck in the Belgian paper *La Cigale*, which claims to be an organ of the "International", a sort of "comic" paper, the like of which certainly cannot be found anywhere else in Europe. There is, you see, nothing comic about it except its seriousness. From the *Cigale* the stuff found its way into the *Pays, journal de l'Empire*... Thereupon we – i.e. the General Council – officially announced, in 6 lines in the *Cigale*, that F. Pyat had absolutely no connection with the International, of which he was not even a member. *Hinc illae irae!* This frog-and-mouse war ended when the French Branch rancorously withdrew from us, and it now goes about its business on its own, under Pyat's auspices. They have established here, in London, as a succursale, a so-called German Agitational Association, consisting of a dozen and a half, headed by an old refugee from the Palatinate, the half-crazy watchmaker Weber. Now you know all there is to know about this solemn, highfalutin and important event. Just one thing more. We had the satisfaction that Blanqui,[115] through one of his friends, writing ditto in the *Cigale*, made Pyat absolutely ridiculous, leaving him only the alternative of being either a monomaniac or a police agent.[116]

LA COMMUNE.

FÉLIX PYAT.

Pyat's habit of calling for Napoleon III's assassination at public meetings was typical of a police agent, but not every indiscreet hothead is an agent provocateur and it appears Pyat's radical anarchist politics were genuine enough. Nevertheless, by claiming he and his followers were the real (or continuity) IWMA, Pyat was not just a thorn in Marx's side, his bloodcurdling threats of assassination created very real and wholly unnecessary problems for the IWMA. Public meetings were banned in France and socialists and trades unionists were already under police surveillance and in danger of lengthy terms of imprisonment just for organising working class resistance to wage cuts and infernal working conditions; and in France the IWMA socialist activists did not need or want to have their political work confused by the London French with pointless assassination plots.

Marx's hostility to the London French was noted in the small world of London radical, socialist and labour politics and it is significant that Bradlaugh allowed Pyat and the London French to use the small hall at the Old Street Hall of Science free of charge for their weekly meetings. In light of Bradlaugh's later wholesale denunciations of the Commune for "senseless violence", and his advocacy of step-by-step, constitutional British republicanism, even this minimal support of just providing Felix Pyat and the London French a free meeting hall demands explanation. It was not as if Bradlaugh was unaware that Pyat preached assassination followed by "spontaneous uprisings" which would install a bourgeois republic of meritocratic atheists such as himself. Pyat had actually made himself and his ideas so well known in London and across Europe, that Marx became almost desperate to disassociate the IWMA from him:

> You will recall that the German Workers' Educational Society here has celebrated the June (1848) Insurrection for about 18 years now. Only in the last few years have the French (their society here now exists as the French Branch of the International) taken part. And the old *meneurs* [leaders] always stayed away. I mean the *petits grands hommes*.
>
> But this year, in public meeting, along came Mr Pyat and read out an alleged address of the Paris Commune[117] ... in which the *assassinat* of Bonaparte was preached, as it was years ago in his *Lettre aux étudiants*. The French Branch, reinforced by other bawlers, acclaimed this. Vésinier[118] had it printed in *Cigale* and *Espiegle*, Belgian papers, and presents Pyat as giving his direction to the "International".

As a result, we get a letter from the Brussels committee, which just at the moment is making great propaganda, under difficult circumstances (Charleroi affair). Contents: This demonstration threatens to wreck the entire Association on the continent. Will the French Branch never move forward from the old demagogic phrases, etc.? ... It should be remembered that, at this very time, our people are behind bars in Paris. We yesterday issued a declaration (to be printed in Brussels), disavowing any connection between the above-mentioned Pyat and the International.

Indeed I regard the whole affair (naturally based upon the background of the enormous stupidity of the French Branch) as an intrigue of the old parties, the republican jackasses of 1848, especially the *petits grands hommes* who represent them in London. Our Association is a thorn in their flesh. After trying in vain to work against the Association, the next best thing, of course, is to compromise it. Pyat is just the man to do this *de bonne foi*. The cleverer ones therefore push him forward... The French Branch here will have to be thrown out of the International if it does not put a stop to its asininity. One cannot allow 50 unprincipled louts, round whom loudmouths of all nationalities gather at such public opportunities, to endanger the International Association at a moment when, as a result of conditions on the continent, it is beginning to become a serious power.

Pyat was not the only anarchic revolutionary preaching assassination, Bradlaugh had associated with; some years earlier, after Felice Orsini's[119] failed assassination attempt on Napoleon III, Bradlaugh had been involved in the defence of Simon Bernard, Orsini's bomb-making accomplice in London, as well as the defence of the almost ubiquitous Edward Truelove, who had published a pamphlet in praise of Orsini, *Tyrannicide, is it ever Justifiable?*.[120] At the time, Bradlaugh was still clerk to the future fugitive Montague Leverson, who was Bernard and Truelove's solicitor. Leverson did not usually handle political cases and he probably only took Bernard and Truelove at Bradlaugh's instigation.

No-one remotely on the left would ever weep for the death of Napoleon le petit, but although Marx was approached he kept out of affair:

Please return the enclosed letter from the regicide Simon Bernard. Do you think I should get involved in the matter? I rather think not.[121]

In getting involved, Bradlaugh had less to lose than an alien refugee like Marx, but it is still added something to Bradlaugh's radical credit that he found Bernard such a good defence lawyer in the still young Henry Hawkins (later when a judge known as Hanging Hawkins)[122] that Bernard was acquitted much to his surprise and everybody else's, including Hawkins.

Interesting as the Orsini-Bernard case is, what it reveals is that Bradlaugh supported Napoleon III's would-be assassins as enthusiastically as he would later condemn the "senseless violence" of the Communards. Bradlaugh had not had a change of political heart. In fact, Bradlaugh did not (as he would claim during and after the Commune), object to violence in itself, Bradlaugh objected to Communard violence because it was motivated by socialism, while he condoned Orsini and Bernard because it was motivated by bourgeois republicanism.

Another illustration of Bradlaugh's readiness to tolerate violence if and when it suited his limited radical agenda connects to the IWMA via the Reform League. As part of the campaign for a wider franchise the Reform League decided to organise what they called monster demonstrations in London. Some 200,000 people turned up to the first of these held in Trafalgar Square on June 29th 1866 (just three days after the fall of Lord John Russell's Liberal Government). A second almost equal in size was held on July 2nd 1866, but when a third Hyde Park demonstration was called for July 23rd 1866, the police were ordered by the Earl of Derby's new Conservative Government to deny the demonstrators access to the park.

Tearing down the railings at Hyde Park, 1866

Edmund Beales, President of the Reform League and some of the other leading luminaries were happy enough to give up the idea of the demonstration and spend the afternoon in Gunter's Tea Shop in Berkeley Square, but a large number of demonstrators broke ranks and forced entry into the park by pulling down the railings. Once they were safely down, Bradlaugh, who, it has to be admitted, had not been seduced by Gunter's famous cakes, led one contingent of demonstrators into the park at Knightsbridge; though there is no report of Bradlaugh personally involving himself with pulling down any railings.

There were some clashes between demonstrators and police and though there were no fatalities, there were some serious injuries and while none of the Reform League leadership was arrested, a good many "ordinary" working class men served prison terms with hard labour. The Reform League executive deemed the demonstration a success and it probably was; as it certainly helped both Disraeli and Gladstone to persuade more anti-reform backbenchers to see the merit of allowing some limited extension of the franchise as a way of preventing further riot and mayhem.

By this time, Marx was aware that the Reform League was going to settle for far less than the manhood suffrage they had originally been set up to demand, and Marx, who had truly human, rather than merely ideological, sympathies with the working class, was none too impressed by the newspaper reports of working class demonstrators being imprisoned for a very limited extension of the franchise.

> Meanwhile, whilst these riff-raff (The Reform League leadership) are patting each other on the back and be lick-spitting each other, that cur Knox, the police magistrate of Marylebone, is sending people down in a summary fashion, which shows what would happen if London were Jamaica.[123]

The following summer in 1867, the extension of the franchise was still being discussed by Liberals and Tories alike and the Reform League executive decided to be conciliatory and called for a "promenade", rather than another demonstration to be held on May 6th 1867. However, when it became clear that despite being re-named a promenade, some 200,000 demonstrators intended to come into central London, the government again threatened to barricade Hyde Park. The Reform League executive debated its course of action. Some, including Thomas Hughes MP, wanted to cancel the promenade or demonstration, or at least postpone it, not only to avoid potential violence but because Derby's government was playing carrot-and-stick and had already tabled a new Reform Bill, and to Thomas Hughes's thinking it seemed foolish to risk having heads broken for something that was soon to be granted.

The Reform League minutes for this discussion are vague, but the executive meeting was fully reported in the following issue of its journal, *The Commonwealth* and from other sources it turns out, that among all the executive, Bradlaugh was the most bold in demanding that the promenade-demonstration should go ahead and that the Reformers should meet police violence with more violence.

Just a few days afterwards on April 4th 1867, the General Council of the IWMA also had a meeting. Marx was not present as he was in Germany finalising the publication of *Das Kapital*, but Joseph Dobson Collet,[124] a close ally of Marx, was in the chair. Marx's future son-in-law Paul Lafargue as well as Marx's long-term friend and ally Frederick Lessner were also present. All three men always followed Marx's line (Lessner without even having to be told what it was) and it is certain that their unanimous decision to write to Beales met with Marx's approval.[125] Collet's letter, which appeared in *The Working Man*, May 4th 1867, is rarely quoted, but it is worth reading in full, as much of its contents are unexpected:

> To Edmond Beales, Esq., M. A., President of the Reform League
>
> Sir,
>
> I am sorry; I was not in time at the last delegate meeting to hear your statement about the measures the Executive Committee of the League had adopted to carry out Mr. Cremer's motion, as they had been requested to do on the previous Wednesday.
>
> I find from the "organ of the Reform movement," the *Commonwealth*, that you stated that "the Council of the League, voting upon the resolution of last week, had decided upon holding not a promenade, as it first intended, but a bona fide meeting in Hyde Park on the 6th of May next," and that, "if any riot or disturbance ensued, the blame must rest on the Government." I find it also stated that Mr. Bradlaugh said that "the League had not only called the meeting in Hyde Park, but meant to hold it there, come what might. On this occasion they would not only demand admittance to the Park, but enforce that admittance if required."
>
> I hope, Sir, you will allow me to make a few remarks on this important subject.
>
> I hold that the people have a right to meet in the Park, but I hold also that before such a serious issue as a defiance to the authorities is raised, men should be prepared to act as men and not as bombastic children.

When I proposed some time ago a promenade in Hyde Park on Good Friday I felt convinced that the Government would not, and could not, prevent the people from going into the Park individually and would not even interfere, if, once there, the people held a meeting.

Some of my friends have tested the question and it has been proved that I was right.

Now I believe that when the delegates voted for Mr. Cremer's motion on the 17th inst. their impression was that the same course should be adopted.

From what I have quoted above, from the *Commonwealth*, it would appear that you, with the Executive, are determined to call forth a demonstration similar to that of July last and that if the authorities adopt the same course they did then, either an appeal to force must be the result, or Reformers would have once more to retire. I believe that it would be, not only impolitic, but criminal to bring the question to such an issue as this, and I will give you my reasons:

If the people of this country are really prepared to join issue with the Government, then they have something better to do than to fight their fellow-men of the army and the police about the question of admittance into the Park.

However important the question of the right of meeting may be, if to settle it force must be resorted to and blood spilt, then the people must be prepared either to submit or to destroy the present political fabric.

I think they are not yet ripe for such an issue, and therefore I say that it would be unwise and criminal to necessarily produce violence and bloodshed, to no practical purpose.

Suppose that the Reformers were even to force their way into the Park, what then? Do you think that the Government would stop there?

What if they bring armed force against you? Are you prepared to meet them?

What if Parliament were to pass a bill forbidding meetings in the parks, would you then turn Parliament out?

I conclude by urging upon you to use your influence upon your colleagues of the Council to reconsider a decision, which I do not think they were empowered to take, by the delegates, and simply to invite the Reformers of London to go individually to the Park, avoiding anything that might have the appearance of a defiance, which they are not prepared to support effectively.

When the time comes, if unfortunately it ever should come, that force must be used, I hope the people of this country will be wise enough to discriminate between those who really are their enemies and those of their own ranks and blood whose interests are the same as theirs, although they may for a time be in the ranks of the army or of the police.

It is not against men obliged then to earn their livelihood that the working men ought [to] turn their wrath. I hope they will have more sense than to do that, and that they will strike the evil, at the root.

I am, Sir,

Yours respectfully, Joseph Collet

This letter may seem pusillanimous, just as Marx's refusal to get involved with Bernard may seem pusillanimous, but not only was Bernard's anarchic belief in isolated assassinations wrong-headed, but in 1862 Marx knew that:

> Bernard, always very eccentric and having in any case overworked during the past few weeks, has become subject to "hallucinations".[126]

It was not that Marx was timorously opposed to all violent demonstrations, he was only opposed to those that he thought had little chance of success - and who is to say Marx was wrong? In the 19th century defying a government ban to demonstrate was an enterprise with consequences far beyond the inconvenience of being "kettled".

Granted it was over forty years since the Manchester magistrates had called in the yeomanry to break up a massive demonstration in favour of a wider franchise. But the memory remained of how Orator Henry Hunt was about to address the crowds, when the mounted yeomanry drew their sabres and attacked the gathered workmen and their families. Known to history as the Peterloo Massacre some twenty demonstrators were killed and several hundred more injured. In another twenty years, on November 13th 1887, the Metropolitan Police and Household Cavalry would attack another massive demonstration, this time in Trafalgar Square. There were deaths and injuries.[127] (Marx's youngest daughter Eleanor, by then a socialist activist, got knocked about and bloodied about in the fray).[128] That day was called Bloody Sunday, keeping the title in British memory until the far deadlier events in Derry on 30 January 1972 superseded it.

The right to demonstrate is of course important, but it is not a political end in itself. To paraphrase Marx's dictum, the object of revolutionaries is not to demonstrate against the world, but to change it. In 1867 Marx and his supporters clearly thought like Thomas Hughes that a slightly widened franchise was not worth more injured workers and prison terms; especially as a "moderate"

Bill which most of the Reform League was minded to accept was already wending its way through Parliament. The issue here is not so much whether Bradlaugh was right in calling for riot, or Marx and his supporters were right in calling for restraint, but that Bradlaugh, who would so loudly decry the "senseless violence" of the Commune, when it fought for socialism, was here calling for all-out violence and confrontation in defence of a radical demand for just a tiny little bit more democracy.

There is an intriguing twist to the story.

A Twist of Bradlaugh

Bradlaugh's voice is recorded as being the most vociferous in favour of defying the government's order and forcing entry into Hyde Park no matter what opposition the police or soldiery presented. Yet on the day before the May 6th demonstration, Bradlaugh, without informing anyone on the Reform League's executive, went to the House of Commons seeking a private interview with both the Tory Disraeli, who was Chancellor of the Exchequer, and the Liberal Gladstone, who was out of office. Bradlaugh had no difficulty meeting Disraeli, but he had to content himself with Gladstone's secretary.

Disraeli was always open to meeting reformers and even socialists. In his autobiography, H M Hyndman relates how he spent an afternoon in the early 1880s outlining his Marxist plans to Disraeli,[129] while in his autobiography, George Jacob Holyoake tells of how in the 1840s, he had personally gone to Disraeli to collect money for the London Chartists, an open admission of taking "Tory Gold" which for some reason has never garnered much attention.[130]

Once closeted with Disraeli and Gladstone's secretary Bradlaugh presented himself as the one and only man who could prevent violence. Perhaps the interview had some good effect as the government lifted its ban on entry to Hyde Park and the demonstration passed off peacefully; but some MP friends of Thomas Hughes MP spotted Bradlaugh in the lobby of the House of Commons and finding out Bradlaugh's mission, told Hughes, who went straight to inform the rest of the Reform League's executive.[131] Hughes's revelation caused an outcry. After having been foremost in calling for confrontation, Bradlaugh's secret meeting now gave him the hallmark of the agent provocateur. It played so badly that Bradlaugh had to resign from the Reform League executive.

Bradlaugh's forced resignation rankled with him and he blamed Hughes for it. Some five years later in 1872, it was still rankling, and there was some unpleasant correspondence between Bradlaugh and Hughes which brought in George Howell and Edward Beales, where Bradlaugh tried unsuccessfully to exonerate himself from the charge of double-dealing.[132] Hughes utterly refused to back down and challenged Bradlaugh to take him to court for libel. In his turn, Bradlaugh blustered, imperiously telling Hughes:

> that I require you to submit to a court of honour to be composed of three or five persons...[133]

The suggestion was absurd, and Bradlaugh's grandstanding indicates a self-conceit bordering on the pathological. It would perhaps hardly matter except as a curiosity, except that earlier in the very same year Bradlaugh also challenged Marx to submit to what on that occasion Bradlaugh called a "Council of Honour".

> I offer to submit the whole question between myself on the one side and Dr Karl Marx and the International on the other to a Council of Honour before whom I undertake to reasonably justify all I have written and to furnish much more than the "slightest pretext" for every statement I have made concerning Dr Marx or the society; one condition of the submission being that Dr Marx adopting the acts of his official subordinates of the International undertakes to do at least the same on his part as I do on mine.[134]

Marx was so outraged by Bradlaugh's effrontery that he responded in time to make the second edition of the *Eastern Post*:

> Sir,
>
> In his immortal poem, Dante says that one of the most cruel tortures of an exile is the necessity of having to rub elbows with all sorts of people. I have deeply felt the truth of his complaint when being forced to enter for a moment into a public controversy with men like Messrs. Charles Bradlaugh and Co. I shall, however, no longer allow him to turn the quarrel he has fastened upon me into the cheap and convenient means of advertising himself abroad.
>
> He [Bradlaugh] published against me an accusation which, if published in Germany, would have made him the laughing-stock of all parties; I thereupon challenged him to publish such facts as might have lent him the slightest pretext for a calumny as ridiculous as it is infamous. I did so in order, not to justify myself, but to expose him. With the low cunning of a solicitor's clerk he [Bradlaugh] tries to escape this liability by inviting me to a "Court of Honour."

Does he really fancy that a Bradlaugh, or the editors of the Paris *demi-monde* Press, or those of the Bismarckian papers at Berlin, or the *Tages-Presse* at Vienna, or the *Criminal-Zeitung* at New York, or the *Moscow Gazette*, have only to slander me, in order to make me amenable to clear my public character, and even to do so before a "Council of Honour," of which the friends of those "honourable" gentlemen must form part?[135]

Bradlaugh did not get his "court or council of honour" with Marx, any more than he did with Hughes; even so, the scenario was still a good piece of showmanship on Bradlaugh's part, as he could parade himself in public before his huge secularist and radical audience, as an honest and brave man traduced by enemies too cowardly and unsure of their facts to "meet him" in what he cavalierly argued was the fair fight of a court or council of honour.

Bradlaugh's self-regard and arrogance were relentless and over the years it lost him some friends and allies, and there were some serious challenges to his domination of radical secularism. But Bradlaugh managed to face them all down and his individual rivals and opponents either came to heel (the Holyoake Brothers,[136] G W Foote) or, they were disappeared out of radical secularism. (Harriet Law, James Thomson,[137] Dr Edward Aveling), while any secularist organisation set up in opposition to Bradlaugh always floundered. From the General Secular Reformers' Society to the British Secular Society; (briefly headed by the quixotic Marquess of Queensbury, who established the Queensbury rules for boxing and later baited Oscar Wilde to his final destruction), all the way down to Edward Aveling's more humble attempt to set up a rival secularist base in North London, each and every attempted secularist *coup d'état* against Bradlaugh met with failure. This raises the question not just about Bradlaugh's charisma, but his funding.

Bradlaugh might have made enemies over the years, and he fought many court cases, and while his friends claimed he died poor, he actually left over £4000, a very decent sum of money for an allegedly poor man Yet Bradlaugh's funding, unlike Howell's, remains obscure.

What is clear is that Bradlaugh developed an extensive network of friendships including friendships with many of the joint members of the Reform League and the IWMA, who he would often meet up with on the Monday or Tuesday evening just before the weekly IWMA General Council meeting.

Gradually, but noticeably all the prominent trades unionists, with whom Bradlaugh retained good relations, who served on both General Council and the Reform League executives deserted the IWMA (not just Cremer, Odger and Lucraft, but Buckley, Blackmore, Coulson, Dell, Hartwell, Howell, Leno, Longmaid, Osborne, Stainsby and Wheeler) and while they were replaced, very few of the new General Council members were prominent trades unionists.

These defections from the General Council often arose over disagreements with Marx; for while Marx defeated the Mazzinistas, Proudhonistes and ultimately the Bakunistas, the essential radical mindset of the majority of early General Council members was not won over to Marx or socialism. Bradlaugh's anti-trade unionism might not attract them, but in every other particular, even Malthusianism, they found they had much more in common with the meritocratic and class collaborationist ideas of Bradlaugh than they ever did with Marx's "foreign" ideas of class struggle and the intrinsic exploitation of capitalism.

Marie Joseph Louis Adolphe Thiers (from portrait by Disdéri)

The "Mohr - Bradlaugh Affair"[138]

Bradlaugh's background and subterranean hostility towards Marx only broke cover in 1871 over the Commune of Paris and Marx's defence in *The Third Address on the Civil War in France*; without such momentous events, it may just have simmered in the background. Having broken cover, only Abramsky and Collins among serious historians go into much detail about the Mohr-Bradlaugh Controversy,[139] and even they suggest that the "machinations" of Maltman Barry[140] within the International were "much more dangerous" to Marx than the antagonism of Bradlaugh.

The Commune of Paris

For all its faults and ultimate defeat the 1871 Commune of Paris was the greatest revolutionary event in Europe between the French Revolution of 1789 and the Russian Revolution of 1917. France had its revolutionary opportunity through its military defeat by Prussia in 1870. Napoleon III, having escaped Felice Orsini's bombs and Felix Pyat's wild threats, found himself defeated in the field and taken prisoner by the Prussians at Sedan. His throne did not survive his humiliation and on September 4th 1870, a provisional Government of National Defence was declared; to be followed by elections by the grace of the occupying German Army. A mixed bourgeois republican and monarchist assembly was returned and "that mysterious abortion"[141] Adolphe Thiers, "consistent only in his greed for wealth and his hatred of the men that produce it",[142] became President of Third French Republic at the beginning of 1871: Marx's description of him is as Lord Salisbury said elsewhere, a wonderful display of invective:

> Thiers, that monstrous gnome... A master in small state roguery, a virtuoso in perjury and treason, a craftsman in all the petty stratagems, cunning devices, and base perfidies of parliamentary warfare; never scrupling, when out of office, to fan a revolution, and to stifle it in blood when at the helm of the state; with class prejudices standing him in the place of ideas, and vanity in the place of a heart; his private life as infamous as his public life is odious...[143]

Marx was equally contemptuous of Jules Favre, the new foreign secretary:

> Jules Favre, living in concubinage with the wife of a drunken resident at Algiers, had, by a most daring concoction of forgeries,

spread over many years, contrived to grasp, in the name of the children of his adultery, a large succession, which made him a rich man, and that, in a lawsuit undertaken by the legitimate heirs, he only escaped exposure by the connivance of the Bonapartiste tribunals...[144]

Bradlaugh would attack Marx for making what he considered personal attacks, or called dealing in "personalities", but then Bradlaugh's view of the men of the Third Republic was very different from Marx's. The very day after Blanqui attempted a coup in besieged Paris,[145] Bradlaugh contacted Favre through Charles Tissot, the new republic's chargé d'affairs in London. Bradlaugh's words are very suggestive:

> ...my head, tongue, pen and influence, which unfortunately are all I have to offer, you may use, but to use them really effectually I must understand distinctly how and to what extent you want me to work... My friends throughout Britain you can count on as yours...[146]

Tissot wrote enthusiastically to Favre about the size and importance of Bradlaugh's radical following; perhaps he exaggerated, as Tissot described Bradlaugh's Old Street Hall of Science, not only as always full to overflowing, but as having seating for one thousand four hundred and fifty people, and whether Tissot thought Bradlaugh was actually useful enough to fund is a detail lost to history, still Bradlaugh's offer of total and unquestioning support to a newly installed foreign government ("The National Government for the Defence of France") remains striking and suggestive.

It was not until late January 1871 that Thiers and Favre agreed an armistice with Bismarck and after one hundred and thirty eight days, ended the siege of Paris. The terms of peace were harsh. The French were to pay huge reparations, while a vast area of Alsace Lorraine was to be ceded to the new united and Imperial Germany. Apart from the injustice of giving several million people as a trophy to a conqueror, the reparations were obviously going to be a huge burden on French workers. It was true that the war had replaced the monarchy with a republic, but Thiers, Favre and their coterie of opportunists had no plans for social reforms of any benefit to the working people of France, the new republic was merely the change-over from one ruling elite to another, or as Marx would say "a mere shuffling of the cards".

The reaction of the people of Paris was to rise not merely in revolt but in revolution. Twenty years later, Engels still thrilled at the Commune's greatest if short-lived achievement: "The Dictatorship of the Proletariat... do you want to know what this dictatorship looks like? Look at the Paris Commune. That was the Dictatorship of the Proletariat."[147] In *State and Revolution*, Lenin agreed, picking out in particular how the Commune was:

> ...a working, not a parliamentary body, executive and legislative at the same time ... all officials without exception, elected and subject to recall at any time, their salaries reduced to working men's wages, these simple and self evident democratic measures which completely uniting the interests of the workers and the majority for peasants, at the same time serve as a bridge leading from capitalism to socialism.[148]

In the midst of events, Marx wrote more emotionally to his friend Kugelmann:

> ...what historical initiative, what a capacity for sacrifice in these Parisians! After six months of hunger and ruin ... they rise, beneath Prussian bayonets, as if there had never been a war between France and Germany and the enemy were not at the gates of Paris. History has no like example of a like greatness... the present rising in Paris – even if it be crushed by the wolves, swine and vile curs of the old society – is the most glorious deed of our Party since the June (1848) insurrection in Paris... these Parisians, storming heaven...[149]

But writing to Engels, Marx was far less ecstatic. Much as he and Engels would have liked reality to be otherwise, from the outset they both knew the Commune was doomed to military defeat. The *fédérales* (National Guard) in Paris, who had gone over to the Commune, were no match for the forces that Thiers and Favre in collusion with Bismarck would be able to throw against them.

Bismarck no more wanted a social revolution in defeated Paris than he wanted a social revolution in Berlin and even while the German Army was still in France, he released the captured French Army so that it could attack Paris. And if this soldiery had proved incapable of defeating the Commune, Bismarck would have besieged Paris again. Engels had understood this some months before. In September 1870, in a letter to Marx, Engels had all but prayed that Paris would not rise:

> If anything at all could be done in Paris, a rising of the workers before peace is concluded should be prevented. Bismarck will soon be in a position to make peace, either by taking Paris or because the European situation obliges him to put an end to the war. However the peace may turn out, it must be concluded before the workers can do anything at all. If they were victorious now – in the

service of national defence – they would have to inherit the legacy of Bonaparte and of the present lousy Republic, and would be needlessly crushed by the German armies and thrown back another twenty years. They themselves can lose nothing by waiting. The possible changes of frontier are in any case only provisional and will be reversed again.[150] To fight for the bourgeoisie against the Prussians would be madness. Whatever the government may be which concludes peace, the fact that it has done so will eventually make its existence impossible, and in internal conflicts there will not be much to fear from the army, returned home after imprisonment. After the peace all the chances will be more favourable to the workers than they ever were before. But will they not let themselves be carried away again under the pressure of the external attack, and proclaim the Social Republic on the eve of the storming of Paris? It would be appalling if as their last act of war the German armies had to fight out a battle with the Parisian workers at the barricades. It would throw us back fifty years and delay everything.[151]

Engels and Marx were clearly correct in their analysis of the balance of military forces. While the *fédérales* who had gone over to the Commune and the armed Parisians themselves could keep the army of Thiers and Favre at bay, as it turned out, for some two months, the balance of forces meant the military defeat of insurgent Paris was inevitable; however the massacres of some twenty odd thousand Communards and ordinary Parisians which followed that defeat were not. But even before the final collapse, as each barricade was taken, the *fédérales* and the other defenders, male or female, were summarily shot by Thiers and Favre's army. And after the fall of the Commune, even the reports which appeared in a largely hostile British press were unable to disguise the full horrors:

> The column of prisoners halted in the Avenue Uhrich, and was drawn up, four or five deep, on the footway facing to the road. General Marquis de Gallifet and his staff dismounted and commenced an inspection from the left of the line. Walking down slowly and eyeing the ranks, the general stopped here and there, tapping a man on the shoulder or beckoning him out of the rear ranks. In most cases, without further parley, the individual thus selected was marched out into the centre of the road, where a small supplementary column was thus soon formed... A mounted officer pointed out to General Gallifet a man and woman for some particular offence. The women, rushing out of the ranks, threw herself on her knees, and, with outstretched arms, protested her innocence in passionate terms. The general waited for a pause, and then with most impassable face and unmoved demeanour, said:

"Madame, I have visited every theatre in Paris, your acting will have no effect on me." (ce n'est pas la peine de jouer la comedie)... It was not a good thing on that day to be noticeably taller, dirtier, cleaner, older, uglier than one's neighbours. One individual in particular struck me as probably owing his speedy release from the ills of this world to his having a broken nose... Over a hundred being thus chosen, a firing party told off, and the column resumed its march, leaving them behind. A few minutes afterwards a dropping fire in our rear commenced, and continued for over a quarter of an hour. It was the execution of the summarily-convicted wretches.[152]

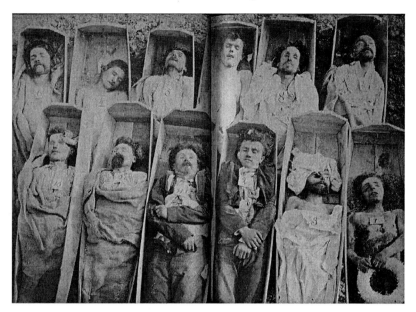

Massacred Communards, 1871

This summary "justice" continued for about a week after the last barricade had fallen; then to quieten mounting international outrage, trials of sorts began to be staged. Initially this only delayed executions by a few hours, but once it was known that the most committed socialists had either been killed or had managed to escape, hulks were arranged to transport those condemned to the living death of life imprisonment on a variation of Devil's Island, Louise Michel among them.

The Communards had also inflicted fatalities of course. For very understandable reasons they shot the Bonapartist, General Lecomte. In Marx's words:

General Lecomte, had four times ordered the 81st line regiment to fire at an unarmed gathering in the Place Pigalle, and on their refusal fiercely insulted them. Instead of shooting women and children, his own men shot him.[153]

The Communards also shot General Clement Thomas, who:

> felt quite proud of having reconquered his June (Revolution of 1848) pre-eminence as the personal enemy of the working class of Paris. Only a few days before March 18, he laid before the War Minister, Leflot, a plan of his own for finishing off *la fine fleur* [the cream] of the Paris canaille.[154]

And rather unwisely and not without internal opposition, the Communards shot the Archbishop of Paris who had been taken hostage along with several other priests, as the Communards had hoped to exchange the Archbishop for the imprisoned Louis Auguste Blanqui, President-elect of the Commune in absentia.

Blanqui had been captured after his abortive coup of October 31st 1870. Later when Thiers and Favre's troops were taking barricade after barricade and murdering the Communard defenders without mercy, the Commune tried to barter the Archbishop's life for the lives of the captured Communards. To no avail, Thiers and Favre would not make any deal for the Archbishop of Paris, and the old man was finally shot as a reprisal during the very last days of the Commune.

There was no practical advantage in killing the aged Archbishop or his Jesuit companions and while the news of the archbishop's execution might be welcomed by ultra hard-line atheists it certainly did not impress the Irish Catholic immigrant workers in Britain. It did not even go down well with Bradlaugh, who as much as he hated the church, certainly hated socialist violence more. But while there is no denying that there were real victims of the Commune, arguably the Communards had been far too merciful towards their enemies, and, rather than being too ruthless, the Commune had not been ruthless enough. This was certainly Marx's view at the time, it also became Lenin's.

Be that as it may, only a handful of Communards were directly involved in either the deaths of Generals Lecomte and Clement Thomas or in the shooting of the Archbishop and the other clerical hostages; and the thousands of Parisians killed by the army of Thiers and Favre cannot logically or justifiably have been executed as punishment for these deaths. Communards and simple Parisians alike were not massacred because some lawful tribunal had found them guilty of specific murders; they were gunned down for the audacity of making war on capitalism and the ruling class.

Just a few days after the *Semaine Sanglante*, Thiers and Favre issued a decree, blaming the Paris rising on the IWMA and asked all governments not only to arrest any fleeing Communards, but to suppress the IWMA and arrest its members. Yet the Commune had wanted Blanqui not Marx as its leader and out of over a hundred elected members, only some twenty-five were also IWMA members. Among these twenty five there were several strong supporters of Marx, but there were also some equally strong anti-Marxists. Outright and total enemies of Marx's version of socialism played conspicuous and even leading roles in the Commune, Felix Pyat and Pierre Vésinier of the London French had crossed the channel to take part and they took their opposition to Marx (and what they termed his autocratic version of socialism) with them. Pyat was elected a member of the Committee of Public Safety and the best that can be said of the Commune's politics is that all shades of socialist and radical opinion were to be found within it. Marxist or not, from the Commune's announcements of women's equality to its provision of free education; to its banning of night work for bakers to the closing of the pawnshops, all the practical measures the Commune tried to introduce were on the side of humanity and progress. And despite Marx's initial doubts about the wisdom of the uprising, when he wrote *The Third Address on Civil War in France*, Marx had no qualms about defending the Commune wholeheartedly and without equivocation.

When *The Third Address on the Civil War in France* appeared at the beginning of June 1871, the massacres of *Semaine Sanglante* had already reached the press, yet even as the "penmen" of the bourgeois press described the horrors perpetrated on the Communards and ordinary citizens of Paris, they also condemned the Commune and denounced the Communards as rogues, cowards, thieves, rowdies and demagogues. Royden Harrison even claims that *The Army and Navy Gazette* hysterically called for all captured Communards to be vivisected without anaesthetic in the interests of science;[155] even more shamefully, the British working class press was very far from being supportive.

There were some notable exceptions; *The Beehive* rather surprised Marx by publishing a series of articles by Edward Beesley defending the Commune. Another positivist Frederic Harrison also had a sympathetic article published in *The Fortnightly Review*. But among working class papers with any large circulation, only the

Reynolds News defended the Commune with any consistency. Guided, or perhaps better said "manipulated", by the reports appearing in *The Times, The Standard, The Daily News,* and *The Chronicle,* a huge proportion of working class opinion ignored both the massacres and the actual measures and policies the Communards had tried to introduce. The working class press, like the bourgeois press, concentrated its attention on what it deemed the outrage of the destruction of some of Paris's wonderful public buildings. John Ruskin's initial favourable opinion of the Commune turned to outright hostility when he learnt of the destruction of the Tuileries. Such was the strength of the propaganda that Ruskin also put the whole blame onto the defending Communards and none onto Thiers and Favre's relentless bombardment with all the latest military technology at their disposal.

Bradlaugh's *National Reformer* was a little slow to comment. Its first major article on the fall of the Paris Commune appeared on June 11th 1871. It was not written by Bradlaugh but by his current bag-man, the twenty-six year old and equally anti-socialist G W Foote.[156] Foote took an Olympian position. He expressed some sympathy towards the Communards, but he derided their apparent aims and objectives and he passed over the massacres and transportation in hulks to New Caledonia, instead Foote took the standard bourgeois line and like *The Times* and other broadsheets, he loftily deplored the Commune's violence.

Bradlaugh maintained his silence in print until July 9th 1871. By that time Bradlaugh's current friends on the General Council, George Odger and Benjamin Lucraft, had both resigned in disagreement over the support offered the Commune in *The Third Address on the Civil War in France.* These resignations were turned into a propaganda victory by Bradlaugh as he bruited the news to radical and trade union London. This was the cue for Bradlaugh to attack Marx head-on beginning with an article entitled "The Commune":

> An address (*The Civil War in France*) officially declared to be from the pen of Dr Karl Marx, but issued with the authority of the General Council of the IWMA has just been published dealing with the late events in Paris.[157]

This is the same article where Bradlaugh attacked Marx for dealing in "personalities" while ignoring his main arguments. It was always Bradlaugh's technique, whether in print or on the platform, to ignore principles and hone in on incidentals amenable to being twisted.

Yet with his access to the 19th century media of platform and print Bradlaugh was capable of doing immense harm; and after being told the contents of Bradlaugh's speech on December 11th 1871, Marx realised he had to counter Bradlaugh openly – but how? In 1871, Marx had hardly any access to the popular media, he was not a platform speaker, nor were any of his closest allies. His future son-in-law Charles Longuet did challenge Bradlaugh to a public debate,[158] but as for the press, while *Reynolds News* was friendly, only *The Eastern Post* consistently published Marx's letters or reported General Council meetings. It has to be asked, why after living so many years in England, after having been involved at the highest level with the IWMA since its first days, had Marx such little access to the media when he most needed it?

It is easy to suggest that Marx and Engels were boycotted by a bourgeois press which did not want to give space to their ideas, but on closer examination there also seems to have been a strong element of what might be called self-boycotting. Early in their exile, Marx wrote to Engels suggesting what amounted to a policy of writing for any paper regardless of its overall political stance, provided their own articles were not mauled:

> ...we have, of course, now reached the stage at which we regard any English newspaper merely as an emporium and it matters not a rap in which of these emporia we display our "articles", *supposé* they are not tampered with...[159]

Earlier on in the same letter, Marx had outlined some concrete proposals:

> What do you think of my brother-in-law Juta's proposal, enclosed herewith, that we should write a monthly article for the *Zuid-Afrikaan* (Cape Town)? Rotten though Juta's French may be, he's a good, sensible chap. If only you and I had set up an English correspondence business at the right moment in London, you wouldn't be stuck in Manchester tormented by the office, nor tormented by debts. Incidentally, I believe that if you were to send military articles to the London papers now, you would, within a few weeks, be able to secure a permanent post which would pay as well as the Manchester business and leave you more spare time. At present the demand for military writers exceeds the supply.
>
> It might even be asked whether *The Times* itself might not be very glad to hook a military collaborator since it is wretchedly served in this respect...[160]

Yet over time, Marx and Engels's attitude changed and they slowly stopped submitting to papers, not just because sometimes their articles had been altered unacceptably, but sometimes because they simply disliked the paper's overall editorial policy. They sometimes even quarrelled with Ernest Jones and Julian Harney over their more eclectic approach to publishing. And having fallen out with *The Beehive* for its occasional inaccurate and less than supportive reporting of the General Council, Marx was only half joking when he told Edward Beesley, whose pro-Commune articles were appearing in the paper, that:

> Despite my admiration for your article in *The Beehive*, I am almost sorry to see your name in that paper... *The Beehive* calls itself a workers' paper but it is really the organ of the renegades, sold to Sam Morley and Co. During the last Franco-Prussian war the General Council of the International was obliged to sever all connection with this paper and publicly to declare that it was a sham workers' paper. The big London papers, however, with the exception of the London local paper, The Eastern Post refused to print this declaration. In such circumstances your co-operation with the *Beehive* is a further sacrifice you are making to the good cause.[161]

These are just two instances among a general pattern of backing away from relationships with editors and newspapers, which though not completely hostile were not completely supportive either. It was a policy which left Marx without a platform when he most needed one. And in the crisis of 1871 and 1872, all Marx could do to counter Bradlaugh was to write to the editor of *The Eastern Post*. It was not anywhere near enough.

> Sir,
>
> In his last epistle to you, Mr. Charles Bradlaugh makes the report of the sitting of the General Council of December 12th – a sitting from which I was absent in consequence of illness – the pretext for discharging upon me his ruffianism. He says, "I feel indebted to Karl Marx for his enmity." My enmity to Mr. Charles Bradlaugh! Ever since the publication of the "Address on the Civil War in France," Mr. Bradlaugh's voice has chimed in with the world-wide chorus of slander against the "International" and myself. I treated him, like the other revilers, with contemptuous silence. This was more than the grotesque vanity of that huge self-idolater could stand. I "calumniated" him because I took no notice of his calumnies. My silence drove him mad; in a public meeting he denounced, me as *a Bonapartiste* because, in the "Address on the Civil War," I had, forsooth, laid bare the historic circumstances that gave birth to the Second Empire. He now goes a step further and transforms me into a *police agent of Bismarck*. Poor man! He must needs show

that the lessons he has recently received at Paris from the infamous Emile de Girardin and his clique are not lost upon him. For the present, I shall "betray him" to the German public by giving the greatest possible circulation to his epistle. If he be kind enough to clothe his libels in a more tangible shape, I shall "betray him" to an English law-court.

I am, Sir,

Yours obediently,

Karl Marx[162] December 20th 1871

Followed by:

Sir,

In *The National Reformer* of January 7th, Mr. Charles Bradlaugh says: "We only meant to allege that Dr. Marx had, in former times, given information to his own Government."

I simply declare that this is a calumny, as ridiculous as it is infamous. I call upon Mr. Bradlaugh to publish any fact that could afford him even the slightest pretext for his statement. For his personal tranquillity I add that he shall not be "challenged."

I am, Sir, yours obediently,

Karl Marx[163] January 16th 1872

These sharp exchanges between Marx and Bradlaugh were only a part of a lengthy exchange which included letters from several of Marx's supporters on the IWMA including Auguste Serraillier, George Harris, Charles Longuet and the current General Secretary, John Hales,[164] while Victor Le Lubez strenuously defended Bradlaugh. Throughout the winter of 1871-1872, *The Eastern Post* published this acidic Marx-Bradlaugh correspondence alongside reports on the meetings of the General Council and the new local IWMA branches which Marx (under a great deal of pressure headed by John Hales) had finally agreed to set up.

The angry and insulting correspondence sits uncomfortably alongside the Panglossian reports of the IWMA meetings (both in Britain and abroad), where all is presented as going along splendidly:

...The Secretary for Poland reported that he had received news from Cracow. There the Social Democrats had held a meeting and had declared themselves enthusiastically in favour of the international.[165]

...A letter was received from Huddersfield asking for information as to the best means of setting up a branch of the international.[166]

Very little was said about any activities rather than mere messages of support and solidarity, but just occasionally there was a call to action:

> From the Liverpool branch a report was received which stated that the branch was making progress in spite of the reactionary nature of the town... In conclusion the writer urged the necessity of a lecturer being appointed to visit the different branches and asked if the branches in the north could not co-operate for the purpose. It was hoped that the Manchester section will do what it can in the matter.[167]

This was a clear call for the newly inaugurated branch system of the IWMA in Britain to emulate Bradlaugh's propaganda successes by setting up a new national lecturing circuit for socialism in effective competition to Bradlaugh's well-established national lecturing circuit for radical secularism. It was too late, the energy had gone out of the IWMA, the defections and the black propaganda had been too intense and too successful, and without a General Council with the ability to keep a firm grip, a new lecturing circuit could well have fallen into the hands of the radical anti-socialists.

The IWMA was dying as a socialist organisation, and in September 1872, Marx and Engels gave it the *coup de grâce* at The Hague. Generally presented as a massive defeat of Bakunin, The Hague was also a retreat from the battlefield of British anti-socialist radicalism. The soon-to-be-disbanded Liverpool branch of the IWMA would have to wait another twenty years for any kind of socialist lecturer.

Conclusion

Unfortunately, when Marx announced:

> I have done with Mr. Charles Bradlaugh, and leave him to all the comforts he may derive from the quiet contemplation of his own self.[168]

Charles Bradlaugh had not done with Karl Marx, and more importantly what Charles Bradlaugh represented had not done with what Karl Marx represented. For while Bradlaugh the man may be largely forgotten, his bourgeois reformist and meritocratic politics live on and flourish in varying guises in all the main political parties of contemporary Britain; while socialism (let alone communism) seems even further away than it must have done to Lenin in September 1915 when at the Second Zimmerwald Conference he reputedly said in a passing moment of irony that "the Revolution" would not come in his lifetime.

Aftermath: Bradlaugh's very own IWMA

At The Hague Congress in 1872, Marx and Engels successfully managed to move the General Council of the IWMA from London to New York. Often heralded as an astute move, it was rather more an unfortunate, but necessary one. The effort of keeping the IWMA on a socialist let alone a Marxist path had proved too time and energy consuming for Marx and Engels. After The Hague, John Hales tried to establish a British Federal Council of the IWMA to establish the network of local British branches he (and others) had long argued were essential, but as we have seen these came to nothing. The newly established New York General Council also tried to function but by 1876 the IWMA had clearly disintegrated as any kind of organised and coherent force national or international force. This story is well known and often told, what is not well known, and has rarely (if ever) been told is the story of Bradlaugh's attempt to create his own phoenix IWMA out of the ashes of what he dubbed the "Old International".

Bradlaugh's brand-new IWMA also foundered, but the very fact that he attempted to set one up at all, gives considerable weight to the suspicion that Bradlaugh had long coveted control of the original IWMA and that when he realised that this was impossible he became a very determined and consistent enemy of Marx and the First International.

Bradlaugh's *National Reformer* is currently the most detailed surviving source for Bradlaugh's attempt to set up a new IWMA, others may surface.

From late 1877, when Bradlaugh's time was less consumed by the furore of *The Fruits of Philosophy* trial and its aftermath, *The National Reformer* began to mention the idea of a revived international. A full report of an inaugural meeting, headlined "The New International", appeared in its December 16th edition of *The National Reformer*. Several former members of the original General Council are recorded as being actively involved including Marx's long standing but estranged friend, Johann Eccarius[169], as well as Hermann Jung[170], John Hales, John Weston (who had defended the "Iron Law of Wages" against Marx on the General Council in 1865) , Mrs Harriet Law and E Delahaye. Bradlaugh was in the chair and Annie Besant and Edith Simcox[171] were active participants.

A fully attended and representative meeting was held at the rooms of the Women's Provident and Protective League, Little Queen St, High Holborn,[172] to receive the report of the committee set up on the 15th November to draw up the basis of an International Labour Union. Soon after half past eight the meeting was opened, Mr Charles Bradlaugh being unanimously voted to the chair.

The secretary, Mr Pape reported the contents of a few letters and Mr Jung then read the report of the committee and moved its adoption in an able and sensible speech, pointing out the need for such an organisation as was proposed. He considered that the plan now being adopted towards the masons was now likely to be extended to other trades and it was therefore most important that English trades unionists should act in harmony with foreign workers and prevent the employers from playing off one country against the other.

Mr Ackrill seconded the adoption of the report urging the need for an international organisation.

The secretary then read the following, a copy of which had been given to each individual present.

A meeting was held at the Women's Provident and Protective League on the 15th November 1877 for the purpose of considering the advisability of forming an association to secure the better international understanding in the interests of labour; when it was unanimously declared to be advisable to establish and English branch of an international Labour union to unite in fraternal bond the workers of different countries.

A committee of nine was then appointed who have unanimously agreed to recommend the following propositions to then next meeting.

1st That the title of the organisation should be the International Working Men's Association.

2nd That the objects of the association be to unite in fraternal bond the workers of all countries and to afford a medium of information and assistance for their common interests.

3rd that the association shall form an international agency between the different national and local organisations so that the workers in one country be constantly informed of the movement of their class in every other country; that an inquiry into the social state of the different countries be made under common direction; that the questions of general interest mooted in one society be ventilated by all; and when immediate practical steps should be needed, as for instance, in case of international complications, the actions of the associated societies should be simultaneous and uniform

4th that since the success of the working class movement in each country cannot be secured but by the power of union and combination, the Association shall use its influence to organise the workers into trade societies and Labour Unions.

5th that any person may become a member of the Association by adopting its principles and conforming to its rules.

6th that any society of Workers may join the association by Adopting its rules and Principles and by declaring its adhesion to the same and forwarding its regulations and bylaws (if any) for approval.

7th that the management of the Association be vested in a council which shall form a bureau of correspondence and be charged with the collection of statistics bearing on the condition of the working classes

Signatures

Ackrill, J Hales, (Alsagar Hay) Hill, S D Headlam,[173] H Jung, McGiffin, Edith Simcox, Schuman, Weiler, Fletcher Pape (Hon Sec)

Mr Delahaye (France) thought that the prospectus was too vague and urged that the basis should be economical and not political. None of the great trade societies in France had ever as such joined the Old International, even when it was at its highest point of numbers. Workers were too divided in politics to unite in political action and each country had its separate political needs, but they might all unite on an economical basis, their interests being the same. Definite proposals should be made, for instance, for a uniform numbers of hours for the working day.

The Chairman (Bradlaugh) suggested that it would be wise to take the propositions one by one and a general assent was expressed. On clause 1 being read, moved and seconded.

Mr Hales prefaced his remarks by a statement that he had on committee reserved for appeal to the meeting the 1st clause moved as an amendment that the name of the organisation should be "The International Association for Promoting the Interests of Labour". To call the new union by the old name would be thought be a fatal blunder. It was better to avoid the old prejudices. Besides the name seemed to exclude women.

Mr Van de Hout seconded the amendment

The Chairman (Bradlaugh) remarked that the name proposed would in two countries at least, subject members to arrest without warrant, and it was well that that fact should be known.

Mr Alsager Hay Hill supported the amendment thinking that the old name might be misunderstood.

Mr Weiler thought it was a matter of perfect indifference whether they affronted prejudice or not. The society was sure to be opposed whatever name it took, because any society in the interests of labour would be hated and opposed. The name wouldn't interfere with women joining as it was easy to introduce a rule stating that "men" was intended to include women.

Mr Ford supported the amendment so as to avoid old prejudices and any conflict with the laws of foreign countries. The inclusion of women in such a scheme was most necessary. He would prefer some such word as cosmopolitan to that of international.

Mr Macara supported the amendment as "working men" was too narrow a phrase and seemed to exclude all save artisans-manual labourers.

Miss Simcox supported the original resolution considering that "men" included women and was simply sued as a generic name for all human beings. They ought certainly to keep the term international, and though the object before them might be hard to gain, all great things were difficult of attainment and needed courage and steadfastness of purpose to achieve them.

Mr Howell would prefer a shorter name such as International Labour Association

Mr Weston would keep the old name.

Mrs Besant supported the amendment; she thought that the prejudice that might be excited by the old name did not matter, as the prejudice was against the work not the name, and any society that did good work for the oppressed would be hated by those whose interests lay in the oppression. But the term "men" was too exclusive. It would be taken as meaning men, and the women who might be admitted by a special rule would be an excrescence, not part of the original society. She urged the new association to stand on higher grounds, than the old one and be as much against distinctions of sex as above distinctions of class.

Mr Headlam supported the amendment on the same ground

Mr Hales explained that the prejudice he alluded to was among the workers not the employers. He was not ashamed of the old name, but he did not want the old quarrels revived.

Mr Jung, in reply urged that the amendment was unnecessary and that women were included; in fact in the old international, a woman (Mrs Law) sat on the council. "Workmen" did not only mean artisans, and as to the penal laws, the work was what was objected to, and the laws would be very easily altered to apply to the new association, whatever name it might near. There was really no dear of the old and new association being confused and the trades unions were not prejudiced against the old society.

A show of hands being taken, the amendment was carried 23 against 22

The chairman (Bradlaugh) said the majority was so small for so important a matter, that perhaps it would be well to vote again, sitting and standing

The amendment was then lost 24 to 22

An amendment was moved and seconded that the society be called the International Labour Union and was carried 25 to 16.

It was then put as a substantive motion and carried with two dissentients.

Paragraphs 2,3,4,5,6,7 were then severally moved an seconded and were agreed to without discussion

Mr Hales proposed and Mr Grout seconded that Mr Pape be appointed secretary pro tem.

Mr A. H. Hill proposed that the provisional council be appointed to draw up the rules of the union to be submitted to a future meeting and Mr Hales suggested that it should be composed of 21 members. Agreed to. Twenty seven names were proposed and voted on by show of hands, the following being elected: [ex General Council members in italics]

Mr Jung 40, Mr Bradlaugh 37, *Messrs Hales*, *Weston* and Miss Simcox 35 each, Mrs Besant 34, Mr Headlam 33, *Mr Eccarius* 30, Messrs Hill, Van der Hout and *Mrs Law* 28 each, Mr Brown 27, Mr Ackrill 26, Mr Foster 24, Mr Shipton 22, Messrs Grout and Hodgeson Pratt 20 each, Messrs Barvis, Kean Shuman, *Delahaye* and Howell[174] obtained 19 votes each, and the four first were elected on a second vote being taken.

The meeting was then adjourned to that day six weeks, votes of thanks being passed to the chairman (Bradlaugh) and to the Women's Provident and Protective League (Edith Simcox).

Despite Bradlaugh's best efforts via Besant, his wish to have the new organisation called the International Working Men's Association was rejected, and Bradlaugh's intended continuity (or coup) has probably been overlooked because a new name, the International Labour Union, was chosen. Even so there can be no doubt that with himself at the helm Bradlaugh's intention was to resurrect the old IWMA, but as a new anti-socialist, class collaborationist body.

In the name of women's equality, Annie Besant and Edith Simcox were both furiously opposed to Marx and Engels's variously expressed support (purely on health grounds) for women's work to be more restricted than men's, and inevitably they saw a restructured IWMA-ILU as a vehicle to campaign for their Liberal *laissez-faire* concept of women's liberation as well as Malthusian economics, but they were thwarted. The reconstituted IWLA-ILU failed. Tracing the increasingly intermittent references to the ILU in *The National Reformer* it becomes ever more clear that the ex-General Council members not only began to dominate, but despite their various previous conflicts and disagreements with Marx, many of them were still all far too socialist-minded for Bradlaugh to tolerate (in particular Mrs Law and Hales).

While *The National Reformer* continued to feature articles blaming the high working class birth rate for poverty and decrying strikes as pointless as they went against the Iron Law of Wages, the ILU offered its support to the Lancashire cotton strikers[175] and point blank refused to support Malthusian explanations for poverty, even when appealed to directly by Mrs Besant.

> [The ILU executive council] expresses support for Mrs Annie Besant in having lost [custody of] her child for her Malthusian and anti-theological views however the (ILU executive) council expresses no opinion on those principles. It [merely] protests against the [court's] decision[176] on the ground that liberty of opinion should be perfectly free.[177]

Even more disappointing for Bradlaugh, the new ILU was as angered as Marx by George Howell's July 1878 article attacking Marx in the *Nineteenth Century*. *The National Reformer* reports:

> A spirited discussion [at the ILU executive] relative to Mr Geo Howell's article in the 19th century... [it] was unanimously condemned and Mr Jung at the request of the [executive] signified his willingness to prepare a reply thereto.[178]

It was while she was sitting on the ILU executive that Mrs Law offered Marx a platform in her weekly *The Secular Chronicle* to rebut Howell's mendacious accusation that it was Marx who introduced "the religious idea" (or atheism as an ideal) into the IWMA. Bradlaugh could hardly have endured to see such support regrouping for a man and an ideology he must have thought he had beaten into oblivion.

The end came quickly when the ILU executive, under Hales and Law's influence, voted to establish a provincial lecturing circuit to preach a version of socialism in direct conflict with Bradlaugh's radical self-help individualism. With this threat in view, Bradlaugh withdrew his interest and without an office and funding the ILU disappeared – but by then the socialist revival of the 1880s could almost be felt in the air.

Notes

1. John Spargo 1876-1966, born in Cornwall, stonemason by trade. He was initially active in the SDF. He emigrated to America where he was considered a leading socialist until the First World War which he supported. Spargo opposed the Bolsheviks in 1917; he thereafter joined the Republican Party and supported Calvin Coolidge.

2. Laura Lafargue, née Marx, 1846-1911, married Dr Paul Lafargue in 1868. Lafargue, a Cuban-Frenchman, came under Marx's influence in 1866 when he served as a member of the General Council of the IWMA; he was corresponding secretary for Spain. A somewhat maverick Marxist, he was a founding member of the French Workers' Party and served as deputy for Lille. The Lafargues' three children died in infancy.

3. Paul and Laura Lafargue were in Bordeaux, not Paris, during the Commune, but Lafargue went to Paris to take instructions and attempted to set up a revolutionary Commune in Bordeaux.

4. Vladimir Lenin, *Collected Works*, Progress Publishers, 1974. Lenin's speech at the graveside of Laura and Paul Lafargue also appears in *Sotsial-Demokrat*, No. 25, 8 (21) December 1911.

5. John Spargo-Laura Lafargue Correspondence, International Institute for Social History, Amsterdam, Holland.

6. Mazzinista, follower, or admirer of Giuseppe Mazzini 1805-1872, an Italian bourgeois republican "patriot" involved in the Risorgimento, he spent several years in exile in London, where he was greatly respected by British radicals.

7. Proudhoniste, follower of Pierre-Joseph Proudhon, 1809-1865, who favoured workers' co-operatives and credit unions, opposed strikes as self-defeating and the idea of mothers working outside the home. Marx's *The Poverty of Philosophy* was written as an attack on Proudhon's *The Philosophy of Poverty*.

8. Bakunista, follower of Mikhail Bakunin, 1814-1876, anarchist and serious opponent of Marx within the IWMA; based in Geneva he and his followers were expelled from the IWMA at The Hague in 1872.

9. Austin Holyoake 1826-1874. Secularist, brother of George Jacob Holyoake. Close associate of Bradlaugh and the printer of *The National Reformer*. Involved with the Society for the Promotion of the Employment of Women as well as with Freethought, Austin Holyoake trained women compositors to work on *The National Reformer*.

10. George Jacob Holyoake, 1817-1906. Leading freethinker imprisoned for blasphemy in 1842; a Chartist, he was also heavily involved in the Co-operative Movement. Opposed Bradlaugh over the Knowlton Case and the Oaths Question.

11. H M Hyndman, *Further Adventures of an Adventurous Life*, Macmillan and Co, 1911.

12. John Spargo, *Karl Marx, His Life and Work*, B W Huebsch, New York, 1910.

13. Frederick Lessner, 1825-1910. German-born tailor; member of the Communist League; participant in the Revolution of 1848-49; from 1856 onwards an émigré in London; member of the London German Workers' Educational Association; delegate to the London Conference (1865), the Lausanne (1867), Brussels (1868), Basle (1869) and Hague (1872) Congresses of the International; member of the British Federal Council; founder member of the Independent Labour Party. Good friend of Marx and Engels. One of the four friends of Engels who went out in a boat to throw Engels's ashes out to sea at Beachy Head (the others were Bernstein, Aveling and Eleanor Marx).

14. Frederick Lessner, "A Worker's Reminiscences of Karl Marx", *Die Neue Zeit*, Vol 1, 1923 reprinted in *Reminiscences of Marx and Engels*, Foreign Languages Publishing House, Moscow.

15. Minutes of the General Council of the IWMA, 19 December 1871, Progress Publishers and www. marxists.org.

16. Minutes of the General Council of the IWMA, 19 December 1871, Progress Publishers and www. marxists.org.

17. *The Eastern Post*, 20 December 1871

18. Minutes of the General Council of the IWMA, 19 December 1871, Progress Publishers and www. marxists.org.

19. Montague Richard Leverson, 1830-1891; notice in *The Times*, 1867, revealing that Leverson was wanted by the City of London Police for alleged fraud. Leverson had already absconded to America and never returned to England.

20. The libel was published on 15 August 1868, in *The Razor* edited by J W Marshall

21. *The Razor*, 15 August 1868.

22. *The Times*, 15 January 1869 (Report of the 14 January1869 unsuccessful application by Bradlaugh before Lord Cockburn to have the damages awarded in the original trial increased).

23. Charge of Conspiracy (against Bradlaugh), *The Times*, 15 and 21 September 1864.

24. Karl Marx, *Letters to Dr Kugelmann*, Martin Lawrence undated; Marx to Dr Kugelmann 17 March 1868.

25. In all Marx wrote three addresses on the Civil War in France, the first was published in July1870; the second in September 1870 and the third in June 1871, all references in this article are to the *Third Address on the Civil War in France*.

26. *National Reformer*, 9 July 1871.

27. *National Reformer*, 9 July 1871.

28. *National Reformer*, 9 July 1871.

29. No pictures or plans of the Hall of Science at 142 Old Street have survived but variously in *The National Reformer* for 1868, the auditorium is described as seating 800. Upstairs galleried seating was soon added and most contemporary references have the Hall of Science as seating anything from 1200 to 1450; for example, letter of M Charles Tissot, chargé d'affairs in London (Third Republic), to Jules Favre, 29 November 1870 claims

Bradlaugh's Hall of Science seated 1450 persons and was frequently full; Bradlaugh Collection, folio 219d , Bishopsgate Institute.

30. George Howell, 1833-1910, former Chartist, stonemason by trade, leading trade unionist, Secretary of the London Trades Council (1861-62); member of the IWMA General Council.

31. George Odger, 1813-1877, shoemaker, organizer of Ladies' West End Shoemakers' Society. Member of Reform League executive as well as IWMA.

32. *Third Address on the Civil War in France*, published just after the fall of the Commune in June 1871 as an official IWMA publication.

33. Benjamin Lucraft, 1809-1897; chair-maker. Member of the General Council of IWMA (1864-71), delegate of the Brussels (1868) and the Basle (1869) Congresses of the International; member of the Executive Committee of the Reform League. In 1870 he had been elected to the new London School Board. T H Huxley and Elizabeth Garrett were also elected in the first intake and Lucraft may well have distanced himself from Marx's position on the Commune because of his new LSB membership.

34. *National Reformer*, 24 December 1871. "French Republicanism".

35. Henry Collins and Chimen Abramsky, *Karl Marx and the British Labour Movement*, MacMillan and Co 1965.

36. *The Eastern Post*, radical local Hackney paper which covered the meetings of the General Council of the IWMA.

37. Julius Braunthal, *History of the International 1864-1914*, Vol 1, English translation by Thomas Nelson, 1966. The book also has only one index entry for The Reform League.

38. David McLellan, *Karl Marx*, 1971.

39. National Secular Society website, June 2010.

40. Robert Arthur Talbot Gascoyne-Cecil, 3rd Marquess of Salisbury, (3 February 1830 - 22 August 1903), known as Lord Robert Cecil before 1865 and as Viscount Cranborne from 1865 until 1868. Prime Minister 1885-February 1886 and August 1886 to August 1892 and June 1895 to July 1895.

41. Marx's book was *Herr Vogt*, 1860, a polemic against Karl Vogt, the scientist and erstwhile radical of 1848. It took Marx a year to write, but has only been reprinted as an historical curiosity, Marx, *Herr Vogt*, New Park Publishers, 1982.

42. Karl Vogt was on the Bonaparte payroll. "In the official publication of the list of those receiving direct subsidies from Louis Bonaparte's treasury there is a note that Vogt received 40,000 francs in August 1859. I have informed Liebknecht of the fait, for further use". (The list with details of radical/reformers who were on the Bonaparte payroll had just been published by the Commune of Paris). Marx to Kugelmann, 12 April 1871, published in *Letters to Kugelmann*, Co-operative Publishing Society, 1934.

43. *The Saturday Review*, 19 January 1861.

44. John Rae, 1845-1915. Rae was not a socialist, but an historian and economist best known for his life of *Adam Smith*, MacMillan and Co 1895, Rae also wrote *Contemporary Socialism*, 1887 (a collection of articles which

had appeared in previously in the *Contemporary Review* and *The British Quarterly*).

45. John Rae, "The Socialism of Karl Marx and the Young Hegelians", *Contemporary Review*, October 1881. Marx commented on Rae's article in a letter to Friedrich Sorge dated 15 December 1881. Letters to Americans, International Publishers, 1969: "The English have recently begun to occupy themselves more with Capital, etc. Thus in the last October (or November, I am not quite sure) number of the Contemporary there is an article on socialism by John Rae. Very inadequate, full of mistakes, but 'fair' as one of my English friends told me the day before yesterday. And why fair? Because John Rae does not suppose that for the forty years I am spreading my pernicious theories, I was being instigated by 'bad' motives. 'Seine Grossmuth muss ich loben.' The fairness of making yourself at least sufficiently acquainted with the subject of your criticism seems a thing quite unknown to the penmen of British philistinism."

46. 1887 was the year the "official" Samuel Moore and Edward Aveling translation of *Das Kapital* into English published by Swann Sonnenschein. In sheer desperation to make Marx's work available, just a month after Marx's death, the magazine *Today* published a small excerpt (April 1883) and serialised the first ten chapters in 1885.

47. John Weston, 1810-?; carpenter, subsequently manufacturer. Owenite, participant in the inaugural meeting of 28 September 1864, member of the General Council of the International (1864-72), delegate to the London Conference of 1865; later member of the British Federal Council; one of the leaders of the Land and Labour League. Reform League executive member.

48. The Iron Law of Wages was put forward by the bourgeois economist David Ricardo (1772-1823) and also the non-Marxist socialist Ferdinand Lassalle (1825-1864) and had a real grip on mid-Victorian British radicalism. For some reason there was no Iron Law of Profits.

49. *Socialism Utopian and Scientific* could easily have been available several years earlier, as in 1884 George Bernard Shaw had offered to translate it, but Engels turned Shaw's offer down flat as he had just promised the work to Dr Edward Aveling. Why Aveling took eight years to do the translation is an issue taken up in *Deadly Incubus*, my forthcoming biography of Dr Edward Aveling.

50. The IWMA minutes for 1871 indicate three print runs of 1000, with copies from the third run left unsold.

51. Marx's description, Minutes General Council of IWMA, 19 December 1871, Progress Publishers and www.marxists.org.

52. Apart from bookshops, pamphlets were sold at meetings; for example, *The National Reformer*, 24 December 1871, records twenty political meeting in London, but only one of them dealt with the Commune (It was held at the more socialist-minded Mile End branch of the Land and Labour League. "Mr Weston lectured on the address of the International, (and) many of the addresses were sold."

53. Marx and Engels *Collected Works* Vol 42, Lawrence and Wishart. Marx to Engels, 25 February 1865.

54. Robert Applegarth, 1834-1925; General Secretary of the Amalgamated Society of Carpenters and Joiners (1862-71), member of the London Trades Council; member of the General Council of the International (1865, 1868-72), delegate to the Basle Congress of the International (1869), in 1871. Member of the TUC Junta.

55. Peter Andre Fox, 1831-1869, a Secularist but not an ally of Bradlaugh, one of the editors of *Commonwealth*.

56. Cowen Stepney, dates untraced, apparently a cousin of the 3rd Lord Caernarvon and Auberon Herbert, member of General Council: "A certain Auberon Herbert, brother of the Earl of Carnarvon and cousin to Stepney (who is member of our Central Council) and much dabbling in socialism (i.e., co-operative dodges, etc.), has asked Stepney to arrange a rendezvous with me. As I first want to have sight of the man and smell him over, I have made an appointment to see him next Tuesday at the Cleveland Hall, where we hold our meetings." Letter from Marx to Engels 2 November 1867, Marx-Engels *Collected Works* Vol 42, p. 458.

57. Marx and Engels *Collected Works*, Vol 42, Lawrence and Wishart, Letter Marx to Engels, 6 April 1866.

58. Frederick Engels, *The Labour Standard* 1881.

59. George Grenfell Glyn, 2nd Baron Wolverton, 1824-1887; MP for Shaftsbury, after 1873 sat in House of Lords, parliamentary secretary to the Treasury in Gladstone's first administration and in effect national organizer, Gladstone Papers, British Library.

60. Samuel Morley, 1809-1886; extremely wealthy Liberal "philanthropist", editor of *The Daily News*.

61. Royden Harrison, "The British Working Class and the Election of 1868", *International Review of Social History*, 1961.

62. Northampton was a two-member constituency. In 1880, Bradlaugh was elected junior member, while Henry Labouchère was elected senior member.

63. Henry Bouverie William Brand, later 1st Viscount Hampden after his ancestor the 17th century ship tax rebel, John Hampden. A close friend of Gladstone, Brand came from a very wealthy Liberal family and through his wife Eliza, he was the son in law of Lord Grey, PM at the time of the Reform Act 1832 and the Poor Law Amendment Act 1834. Brand's wife Eliza was the illegitimate daughter of Lord Grey and Georgina, Duchess of Devonshire, friend and political ally of Charles James Fox..

64. Charles Bradlaugh, *The Impeachment of the House of Brunswick*, The Freethought Press, 1872.

65. At one point in the six-year long manoeuvres Bradlaugh was allowed to vote "at his own risk", that is at risk of being privately prosecuted for voting without having taken the oath – which he promptly was, as the litigation and the expense of the litigation was horrendous.

66. *Marx-Engels Correspondence*, International Publishers, 1968. Letter from Marx to his daughter Jenny Longuet, 11 April 1881.

67. Harry Furniss, 1854-1925; Dublin born, Furniss attended the same Methodist School as George Bernard Shaw. Once in London Furniss became a hugely successful illustrator and cartoonist.

68. Harry Furniss, *The Confessions of a Caricaturist*, Vol.1, T Fisher Unwin, 1901.

69. Marx described Gladstone as "that arch hypocrite and casuist" in a letter to his daughter Jenny Longuet, 11 April 1881, *Marx-Engels Correspondence*, International Publishers, 1968 and Marxist Internet Archive.

70. Arthur Wellesley Peel, 1st Viscount Peel, 1829-1912); Peel replaced Brand as Speaker in 1884 and was therefore party to Gladstone's *de facto* policy of keeping Bradlaugh from taking his seat during the Liberal period of office 1880-1886. Peel remained Speaker until 1895.

71. Henry Snell, 1865-1944; initially a secularist, Snell later joined the SDF, then the Labour Party ending up as Leader of the Labour Party in the Lords, as Lord Snell.

72. Snell talking of to the first time he heard Bradlaugh speak at the beginning of the Oaths Question in 1881.

73. Henry Snell, *Men, Movements and Myself*, J M Dent, 1938.

74. Annie Besant, *Autobiography*, T Fisher Unwin, 1893.

75. Thomas Malthus, *An Essay on the Principle of Population*, 1798.

76. Sir Alexander James Edmund Cockburn, 12th Baronet, 1802-1880; Cockburn also summed up favourably in the 1871 transvestite case of Boulton and Parke; the two men were acquitted, however he was brutally anti-working class in his 1877 Woodley v. Metropolitan District Railway Co. judgment and downright unfair in his in 1868 summing up against Michael Barrett, an alleged Clerkenwell Dynamiter and the last man to be publicly hanged in England, *Reynolds News*, 27 May 1868: "Millions will continue to doubt that a guilty man has been hanged at all; and the future historian of the Fenian panic may declare that Michael Barrett was sacrificed to the exigencies of the police, and the vindication of the good Tory principle, that there is nothing like blood". Cockburn also presided over both the civil and criminal Tichborne case.

77. C Kingston, *Famous Judges and Famous Trials*, "Lord Chief Justice Cockburn", Stanley Paul and Co., 1923.

78. Edward Royle, *Radicals, Republicans and Secularists*, Manchester University Press, 1980. Royle argues that Cockburn imposed prison sentences as well as fines on Besant and Bradlaugh because he was annoyed by reports of a speech Besant made on 24 June 1877 at The Hall of Science when out on bail awaiting sentence. Besant truthfully claimed that Cockburn was sympathetic to her and Bradlaugh's Malthusian views and had summed up in their favour. Royle says this public claim was professionally embarrassing to Cockburn, however as the sentences were clearly given in the full knowledge that they would not be served, their harshness is irrelevant.

79. Dealt with under the Writ of Error procedure at The Court of Appeal on 29 January 1878. The legal argument submitted by Besant and Bradlaugh was that while they were charged under the Obscene Publications Act 1857 for publishing *The Fruits of Philosophy*, the particular obscene passages were not published in full in the indictment. Only judges who wanted to

quash a verdict would have found in their favour on such tendentious grounds. (The appeal judges were Lord Justice Bramwell, Brett and Cotton).

80. J B Atlay, *Victorian Chancellors*, Vol. 1 "Lord Lyndhurst", Smith, Elder and Company, 1906.

81. One striking example of a "material fact" used to overturn an actual capital conviction occurred in 1812 when the future Lord Lyndhurst unsuccessfully defended the Luddite John Ingham. Ingham was saved from the gallows on the grounds that the original indictment against him averred he had sent threatening letters to his employers who were the "proprietors of a silk and lace manufactory", when the material fact was that the two named proprietors owned two separate factories, one for lace and the other for cotton. This petty point could easily have been ignored, but the judge in the case allowed it as he did not want to see a man hanged merely for sending a threatening letter. See J B Atlay, *Victorian Chancellors* Vol. 1 "Lord Lyndhurst", Smith, Elder and Company 1906.

82. Truelove also published and sold two other Malthusian birth control pamphlets, written by two other close associates of Bradlaugh, Dr George Drysdale's *Elements of Social Science* and Robert Dale Owen's *Moral Physiology*.

83. William Page Wood, 1st Baron Hatherley, 1801-1881; a first cousin of Annie Besant's father. Lord Chancellor (1868-1872) retired early because he was going blind, not because he had fallen out with Gladstone.

84. Annie Besant repeatedly asserted that Lord Hatherley used his influence to get her husband Rev. Frank Besant the Anglican living of Sisbey in Lincolnshire. See Besant vs. Wood Mabel Besant Custody Trial before Master of the Rolls, George Jessell in 1878 Extra Special Edition *National Reformer*, 1878.

85. Born Katherine Wood, Kitty O'Shea, 1846-1921, was one of Annie Besant's second cousins.

86. Despite always taking the moral high ground publicly, Gladstone long knew of the secret relationship between Kitty O'Shea and Parnell and he often contacted Parnell through Kitty.

87. Besant thought the "safe period" was in the middle of the monthly menstrual period, when (if there is a genuinely safe period at all), it is just after menstruation.

88. The fight against taxes on newspapers (or knowledge) was finally won in 1855.

89. See Marx in *Neue Oder Zeitung*, 28 June 1855, reprinted as "Anti Church Movement. Demonstration in Hyde Park", *Marx and Engels on Britain*, Lawrence and Wishart 1953 and as "Agitation Against The Sunday Trading Bill" in Marx, *Surveys from Exile*, Penguin, 1973.

90. The 1855 Anti-Trading Riots were as successful as the anti-poll tax riot. The proposed legislation was dropped.

91. At the time of the debate (17 April 1884) Hyndman was the leader of the Democratic Federation which changed its name and ethos to the Social Democratic Federation in August 1884.

92. Debate between H M Hyndman and Charles Bradlaugh, held at St James's Hall on 17 April 1884, Professor Beesley in the Chair. Beesley, leading Positivist, Professor of History at University College had chaired the inaugural meeting of the IWMA.

93. H M Hyndman, *Further Reminiscences*, MacMillan and Son, 1912.

94. Hyndman speech in "Will Socialism Benefit the English People" debate April 17 1884.

95. Bradlaugh speech in "Will Socialism Benefit the English People" debate April 17 1884.

96. Long Acre, later the Queens Theatre.

97. Ernest Jones, 1819-1869; barrister and leader of the Chartist movement. At times close to Marx and Engels.

98. IWMA General Council Minutes, 3 October 1865, Howell Collection (Howell 13/1) Bishopsgate Institute.

99. Victor Le Lubez, 1824-1896; French émigré in London, connected radical elements in France and Britain; member of the General Council of the International (1864-66), Corresponding Secretary for France (1864-65), participant in the London Conference of 1865; expelled from IWMA in 1866 at Geneva Congress. Long time member and Treasurer of the National Secular Society, active in both the national and Greenwich branch of the NSS. Close to Bradlaugh. Mazzinista.

100. Karl Marx and Frederick Engels *Selected Correspondence*, Foreign Language Publishing House, Moscow; Lawrence and Wishart c 1953 and Marxist Internet Archive. Marx to Engels, 4 November 1864.

101. *Secular Chronicle*, 4 August 1878.

102. Harriet Law, 1831-1897, married in 1855 to Edward Law, a property dealer. Mrs Law (as she was always called) was brought up as a strict Baptist, but by 1860, she had become the leading female secularist platform speaker. In contrast to most secularists who were pro-science, she had a hobbyhorse dislike of doctors and was in favour of traditional medicine. She had a difficult relationship with Bradlaugh and in 1876 she took over the *Secular Chronicle*. In 1867 she was elected a member of the General Council of the First International, where she invariably supported Marx.

103. George Howell, "The International" *Nineteenth Century*, July 1878.

104. Eleanor Marx-Aveling, "Karl Marx", *Neue Zeit* 1896; Reprinted in *Reminiscences of Marx and Engels*, Foreign Languages Publishing House, Moscow undated.

105. Karl Marx, *Letters to Dr Kugelmann*, Martin Lawrence undated. In a postscript to his letter to Dr Kugelmann dated 11 February 1869, Marx explained, "The cross which my eldest daughter Jenny is wearing in the photograph is a Polish insurrection cross of 1864."

106. Peter Andre Fox, 1831-1869, sometime editor of *The Commonwealth*.

107. The General Council of the IWMA was also sometimes called the Central Council.

108. Marx and Engels *Collected Works*, Vol. 43, Lawrence and Wishart. Letter Engels to Marx 29 November 1869.

109. 1868 saw a General Election which returned the Liberals. Southwark 1869 was a by-election.

110. Letter from Marx to Engels, 2 November 1867, Marxist Internet Archive.

111. Edward Mazzini Truelove, 1849-1917, grew up to reject his Mazzini middle name, changing it to Maurice.

112. Felix Pyat, 1810-1889; journalist, dramatist and political activist. He was also a Freemason in the same lodge of the Philadelphians as Bradlaugh. A defender of regicide and assassination as a political tool, he was more anarchist than socialist. Active in the Commune, he escaped to London. After the 1880 amnesty he served as a deputy in the National Assembly.

113. "Our people", included Longuet and Lafargue.

114. Pierre Vésinier, 1824-1902; a journalist was nominated by Le Lubez and Carter onto the London General Council in September 1865, hostile to Marx, he was expelled three years later. Despite his radical anti-socialism Vésinier had a volatile relationship with Bradlaugh and defended the Commune.

115. Louis Auguste Blanqui, 1805-1881; French socialist who spent altogether 33 years of his life in prison, four of them in solitary confinement. Imprisoned again after an attempted coup against the Third Republic, he was elected President of the Commune in absentia. Blanqui was not a Marxist.

116. Marx and Engels *Collected Works*, Vol. 43, Lawrence and Wishart. Letter Marx to Engels, 5 December 1868.

117. Here, the Paris Commune merely refers to the Municipality of Paris, not the 1871 insurrection.

118. Pierre Vésinier was imprisoned for 18 months in Belgium for violating the press laws in 1866, expelled in 1868; allowed to return to France in 1869, where he was imprisoned in 1870 for the assault on the town hall of Belleville in October 1870. Acquitted in February 1871; Communard, had several functions including editorship of the *Journal Officiel*; contributed to the papers *Le Combat* and *Le Vengeur* of Félix Pyat, founded the journal Paris Libre; fled to England in 1871; chief editor of *La Fédération* 1872; one of the organizers of the anti-Marx Universal Federal Council, returned to France under the amnesty of 1880. He wrote several books on the Commune.

119. Felice Orsini, 1819-1858; executed on 13 March.

120. William Edwin Adams, *Tyrannicide, Is it Ever Justifiable?*, Published Edward Truelove, 1858.

121. Marx to Lassalle 28 April 1862, Marxist Internet Archive.

122. Henry Hawkins 1817-1907; barrister, became a judge of the Queen's Bench in 1876, made Lord Brampton in 1899, died childless and left his fortune to the new Catholic Cathedral in Westminster.

123. Karl Marx and Frederick Engels *Selected Correspondence*, Foreign Language Publishing House, Moscow Lawrence and Wishart c 1953. Marx to Engels, 27 July 1866, Marx is referring to the scandal of General Eyre's brutal repression of the Jamaica Rebellion in 1863.

124. Joseph Dobson Collet 1813-1899, friend of Marx, journalist, writing and editing numerous publications including *Musical World* and *Vanity Fair*. Also sometime editor the *Free Press* and *Diplomatic Review*, *The Working Man* and *The International Courier* (organ of IWMA during 1867).

125. The other General Council members present were Jung, Eccarius, Fox, Hales, Maurice, Carter, Dell, Buckley, and Shaw.

126. Marx and Engels, *Collected Works*, Vol. 41, Lawrence and Wishart. Marx to Engels 27 May 1862.

127. The number of deaths is unknown as for several weeks afterwards there were unsubstantiated reports of men "dying from their injuries".

128. Eleanor's partner, Dr Edward Aveling, managed to escape without a scratch, George Bernard Shaw "skedaddled" to Hampstead and avoided injury. Annie Besant was apparently jostled. Bradlaugh, who had to finally taken his seat in Parliament, was not at the demonstration as he had an urgent lecture engagement in the provinces!

129. H M Hyndman, *Record of An Adventurous Life*, MacMillan and Co, 1911.

130. George Jacob Holyoake, *Sixty Years of an Agitator's Life*, T Fisher Unwin, 1906.

131. The Reform League's executive was gathered at the Reform League's offices in Adelphi Street, making the final plans for the demonstration.

132. Bradlaugh Collection (Folios: 254-255, 258-278) Bishopsgate Institute.

133. Bradlaugh to Thomas Hughes, 7 June 1872, Bradlaugh Collection (Folio 264) Bishopsgate Institute.

134. Bradlaugh to the Editor of the *Eastern Post*, 27 January 1872

135. Karl Marx to the Editor of the *Eastern Post*, 27 January 1872 (2nd edition) and reprinted 3 February 1872.

136. George John Holyoake, 1817-1906, and his brother Austin, 1827-1874.

137. James Thomson, 1834-1882, poet, *City of Dreadful Night*. Thomson was a friend of Bradlaugh from their days serving in the British Army in Ireland. Increasingly alcoholic, Thomson lived in Bradlaugh's house for some time, he translated Heine and Marx particularly admired his translations.

138. Mohr was one of Marx's nicknames, Engels referred to Marx's row with Bradlaugh as the Mohr-Bradlaugh Affair.

139. Henry Collins and Chimen Abramsky, *Karl Marx and the British Labour Movement*, MacMillan and Co, 1965.

140. Michael Maltman Barry, 1842-1909; as a member of the General Council 1871-72, Barry supported Marx, he was also fiercely anti-Russian; in the 1885 General Election he was the conduit for the "Tory Gold" which financed three Social Democratic candidates.

141. Marx to Kugelmann, 12 April 1871.

142. Marx *Civil War in France 1871*.

143. Marx *Civil War in France 1871*.

144. Marx *Civil War in France 1871*.

145. Blanqui and his supporters held the Hôtel de Ville for only one night (October 31st 1870). Defeated, Blanqui was taken prisoner by the Thiers government.

146. Bradlaugh to M Charles Tissot, 1st November 1870, Bradlaugh Collection, (Folio 219a) Bishopsgate Institute. Tissot, 1828-1884, as well as being a French diplomat, later Ambassador to London, was also an archaeologist of North Africa.

147. Frederick Engels, Preface to the 20th Anniversary edition of Marx's *Civil War in France*, 18 March 1891.

148. Lenin, *State and Revolution* 1917 (the two quotes are in reverse order to their appearance in Lenin's pamphlet).

149. Karl Marx, *Letters to Kugelmann*, Co-operative Publishing Society, 1934. Marx to Kugelmann 12 April 1871.

150. Alsace-Lorraine.

151. Engels to Marx, 12 September 1870, Marxist Internet Archive.

152. *Daily News*, 8 June 1871.

153 Marx *Civil War in France 1871*.

154. Marx *Civil War in France 1871*.

155. John Hicks and Robert Tucker, editors, *Revolution and Reaction, The Paris Commune of 1871*, Royden Harrison, *The British Response*, University of Massachusetts, 1971.

156. George William Foote, 1859-1915. In 1883, Foote would be sentenced to a year's imprisonment for blasphemy for some cartoons and jokes he published in his weekly paper *The Freethinker*, which is still published today. In 1891, Foote succeeded Bradlaugh as president of the NSS.

157. *The National Reformer*, 9 July 1871.

158. Letter from Charles Longuet to the Editor, *Eastern Post*, 3 February 1872.

159. Marx to Engels 14 December 1853, Marxist Internet Archive.

160. Marx to Engels 14 December 1853, Marxist Internet Archive.

161. Marx to Beesley, 12 June 1871, Marxist Internet Archive.

162. Marx to Editor, Published in the *Eastern Post*, 23 December 1871.

163. Marx to Editor, Published in the *Eastern Post*, 20 January 1872.

164. John Hales, born 1839, date of death unknown. An elastic web weaver, member of the General Council of the International (1866-72), Secretary (1871-72); member of the Reform League, the Land and Labour League; delegate to the London Conference (1871) and the Hague Congress (1872). By 1872 Hales was vociferously demanding a branch or federal structure to the IWMA and though he supported Marx throughout the entire Bradlaugh-Marx row, he became estranged from Marx over the issue of "federalism" (English provincial branches).

165. "The International Workingmen's Association", *Eastern Post*, 6 January 1872.

166. "The International Workingmen's Association", *Eastern Post*, 13 January 1872.

167. "The International Workingmen's Association", *Eastern Post*, 20 January 1872.

168. Marx to Editor, *Eastern Post*, 28 January 1872.

169. Johann George Eccarius, 1818-1889, member of the League of the Just and later of the League of Communists; member of IWMA from

1864-1872. Long-term friend of Marx, they fell out irretrievably in the dying days of the IWMA.

170. Hermann Jung, 1820-1901, a watchmaker, murdered in his Clerkenwell shop by a young Frenchman who had ostensibly come to him for help. Friendly to Le Lubez who seconded his November 1864 application to join the General Council, Jung also generally maintained good relations with Marx. Jung was president of the Congresses of the IWMA in Geneva, Brussels, Basel and London. Jung remained on the General Council throughout, but in the end supported Hales's idea of a branch or federal structure to the British IWMA.

171. Edith Simcox, 1844-1901; wealthy lesbian trade unionist, she wanted equal pay for women and was opposed to any special treatment, such as shorter hours or a ban on women working nights. In 1875 she and Emma Paterson were the first women to attend the Trades Union Congress as delegates.

172. The Women's Protective and Provident League had been founded in 1875 by Edith Simcox's close colleague Emma Paterson (1848-1886). The League was opposed to any moves to shorten hours or improve working conditions specifically for women, a position shared by Annie Besant, Bradlaugh and the National Secular Society.

173. Rev Stewart Headlam, 1847-1924; an eccentric Church of England clergyman, much to the horror of the Bishop of London, Headlam was a longstanding close ally of Bradlaugh. In 1879, Headlam stood as the obligatory religious reference when Bradlaugh set up evening classes at the Hall of Science (under Edward Aveling's immediate direction). Headlam is perhaps most famous for standing bail for Oscar Wilde and inviting him to stay in his house after Wilde was released from prison.

174. Not the George Howell of the original IWMA.

175. In 1878 the Lancashire cotton operatives were faced with a 10% cut in wages. Bradlaugh argued it was futile for them to strike, the workers argued it was spineless not to.

176. In April 1878, Annie Besant lost custody of her daughter Mabel, after her husband, Rev. Frank Besant successfully argued in court before the Master of the Rolls, Sir George Jessel, that her militant atheism and Malthusian support for birth control made her an unfit mother.

177. *National Reformer*, 26 May 1878.

178. *National Reformer*, 28 July 1878.

THE SOCIALIST HISTORY SOCIETY

The Socialist History Society was founded in 1992 and includes many leading Socialist and labour historians, both academic and amateur, in Britain and overseas. The SHS holds regular events, public meetings and one-off conferences, and contributes to current historical debates and controversies. The society produces a range of publications, including the journal *Socialist History*.

The SHS is the successor to the Communist Party History Group, established in 1946. The society is now independent of all political parties and groups. We are engaged in and seek to encourage historical studies from a Marxist and broadly-defined left perspective. We are concerned with every aspect of human history from early social formations to the present day and aim for a global reach.

We are particularly interested in the struggles of labour, women, progressive and peace movements throughout the world, as well as the movements and achievements of colonial peoples, black people, and other oppressed communities seeking justice, human dignity and liberation.

Each year we produce two issues of our journal *Socialist History,* one or two historical pamphlets in our *Occasional Papers* series, and members' newsletters. We hold a public lecture and debate in London five times per year. In addition, we organise occasional conferences, book-launch meetings, and joint events with other sympathetic groups.

Join the Socialist History Society!
Members receive all our serial publications for the year at no extra cost and regular mailings about our activities. Members can vote at our AGM and seek election to positions on the committee, and are encouraged to participate in other society activities.

Annual membership fees for 2012 (renewable every January):

Full UK	£25.00
Concessionary UK	£18.00
Europe full	£30.00
Europe concessionary	£23.00
Rest of world full	£35.00
Rest of world concessionary	£28.00

For details of institutional subscriptions, please e-mail the treasurer on francis@socialisthistorysociety.co.uk .

To join the society for 2012, please send your name and address plus a cheque/PO payable to **Socialist History Society** to: SHS, 50 Elmfield Road, Balham, London SW17 8AL. Subscriptions can also be paid online. Visit our websites on www.socialisthistorysociety.co.uk and www.socialist-history-journal.org.uk.

Other SHS Occasional Papers for sale

25 Francis King, *The Narodniks in the Russian Revolution: Russia's Socialist-Revolutionaries in 1917*, £5.00

24 Paul Auerbach, Willie Thompson, *Is there No Alternative? Historical Problems of Socialist Economic Strategies*, £2.50

23 Jim Riordan, *The last British Comrade trained in Moscow: the Higher Party School 1961 - 1963* , £2.50

22 Gavin Bowd, *Comintern Cadre: The Passion of Allan Eaglesham*, £2.50

21 Lionel Munby, D Huw Owen, James Scannell, *Local History since 1945: England, Wales and Ireland*, £3.00

19 W Raymond Powell, *Keir Hardie in West Ham: "A Constituency with a Past"*, £2.50

18 Andrew Boyd, *Marx, Engels and the Irish*, £4.00

17 Linda Colley, *Another Making of the English Working Class: The Lash and the Imperial Soldiery*, £2.00

14 Victor Kiernan, *Twenty Years of Europe: The Engels-Lafargue Correspondence*, £2.75

12 Jim Fyrth, *An Indian Landscape 1944-1946*, £5.50

10 Jim Mortimer, *The Formation of the Labour Party - lessons for today*, £2.50

To order these and other SHS Occasional Papers online, please visit http://www.socialisthistorysociety.co.uk/shop.htm. These pamphlets can also be ordered by post within the UK — please send a cheque for the requisite amount (post free) payable to **Socialist History Society**, together with your name and address, to

SHS
50 Elmfield Road
London
SW17 8AL

Socialist History journal

Back copies of *Socialist History*, the SHS journal, are also available for purchase. Nos. 13 to 24 cost £4.50, and nos. 25 to 39 cost £5.50, post free within the UK from the address above. For bulk orders and other enquiries, please contact the treasurer on francis@socialisthistorysociety.co.uk for terms.